IMAGES OF BERKELEY

IMAGES
OF
BERKELEY

RAYMOND W. HOUGHTON
DAVID BERMAN
MAUREEN T. LAPAN

FOREWORD BY
JOHN KERSLAKE

NATIONAL GALLERY OF IRELAND
WOLFHOUND PRESS

Paperback 0 86327 171 5
Hardback 0 86327 176 6

WOLFHOUND PRESS
68 Mountjoy Square, Dublin 1

Design, typesetting and origination by
Printset & Design Limited, Dublin
Printed in Ireland by Criterion Press Ltd., Dublin

COVER ILLUSTRATIONS: Nos. 56, 54 *(Detail)*, 17, 57, 57 *(Detail)*,
56 *(Detail)*, 59, 10, 59 *(Detail)*, 67.

CONTENTS

FOREWORD

A kind of visual *Who was who* of the British achievement, the National Portrait Gallery in London ideally requires of its curators an eye to biography as well as to art, lest they risk becoming experts in faces without knowledge of the men behind them. But with several thousand sitters from the late fifteenth century to the present day ranging from William Shakespeare to Prince William, detailed biographical knowledge is hardly practicable; outside help, especially in remoter disciplines as nuclear physics or philosophy, dare I say it, is both welcome and productive.

A brief note will illustrate how my own experience of Berkeley has been tempered by the findings of others. It began in duty and continued in pleasure. Like his friend Percival, 1st Earl of Egmont, Berkeley's name was listed for inclusion in a new National Portrait Gallery catalogue, (*Early Georgian Portraits,* 1977), begun in the early 1960s. Almost at the outset my sympathy was drawn to that angelic disposition, surely rare in the then higher reaches of the Anglican church; for Atterbury's famous comment had been appended to the back of the Gallery's portrait by an early owner Rev. Thomas Bowdler, 1780-1856. This was almost certainly painted by Smibert, but the date, background and, to some extent, the early provenance were uncertain. W. S. Lewis, the editor of Horace Walpole's *Correspondence* and a good friend of the Gallery, had some years previously sent a snap of Paradise Rock, Rhode Island, taken on holiday by his wife. Smibert's American portraits sometimes incorporated local views, and if the background were Rhode Island, then the portrait would have been painted not in London but on the far side of the Atlantic and after 1728. Correspondence from early owners was received with the portrait and provided a foothold for further research into provenance and condition. Two colleagues at Somerset House kindly led me to the three Berkeley family wills, those of Anne, the bishop's widow; his son George and the latter's wife Elizabeth; also that of Rev. John Kennedy, vicar of Teston, Kent. All had implications for provenance. Meanwhile the scientific department of the National Gallery examined the condition of the paint, including the signature and date, and Dr. Luce wrote from Dublin, encouraging my efforts. Then, by an enormous stroke of good fortune, Sir David Evans walked into my room with the news of the discovery of Smibert's *Notebook.* This contained incontrovertible evidence of 416 portraits, many previously unrecorded, including six of Berkeley, four individual ones and of two, different, groups, though how far some of these correspond with extant paintings is perhaps not yet entirely clear (see below Nos. 10, 20, 21, 26-28). Finally, Dr. Berman now offers the interesting hypothesis that the NPG portrait (No. 20) contains an allusion to Berkeley's running water motif; and the authors suggest that the small Dublin picture (No. 26) is not a copy after, but a study for, the famous group at Yale (No. 27).

From this tercentennial garland, each will gather his favorite image or images. It will be evident that mine have been predominantly visual, though not untouched by biography. I am deeply grateful to the authors for the further aspects of Berkeley here revealed.

JOHN KERSLAKE

PREFACE

How natural it is on significant anniversaries to review personal images from the past. Last year, the tercentenary year of George Berkeley's birth, we had the occasion to rummage through libraries, galleries, books and private collections to review images of Berkeley.

While to reread A. A. Luce's authoritative *Life of Berkeley* (1949) is rewarding, it but stimulates and describes, and leaves to the reader the task of tracing most of the items of interest.

There are the Berkeley portraits, of course, perhaps ten of them executed from life. There are the copies from originals. There are lithographs and mezzotints, and representations that are scarcely more than caricatures. There are sculptures and relief carvings and even a postage stamp.

There are images of his friends Prior, Lord Percival, Swift, Clayton, Johnson and Honyman, of his travelling companions, of his talented and faithful wife, Anne.

There are images of places where he lived, Dysart Castle, and of the only house he ever owned, Whitehall, and of the Palace at Cloyne. There are places he visited in England, Italy and America, and churches in which he preached: St. Colman's in Cloyne, Trinity and St. Paul's in America.

There are things that he knew and owned and sometimes gave away to others: books, Whitehall, medals, poems, a coffee pot.

We wanted to see these things again for study and pleasure and thought that others might wish to do so as well. Aided by a grant from the American Irish Foundation, the assistance of the National Gallery of Ireland, and of Trinity College Dublin, among others, we have arranged an exhibition of the Images of Berkeley at the National Gallery, where a number of original items owned by the Gallery, Trinity College, Marsh's Library and the Royal Dublin Society are shown together with photographs of other pieces from Britain, Ireland and the United States.

There is particular emphasis on Berkeley's experience in America. He devoted ten of his sixty-eight years to his American scheme and was prepared to spend the balance of his life in the New World. The effort was brave and dramatic, and there remains a vital legacy in the cities and educational institutions named after him. His house in Rhode Island remains a living monument to his memory.

We have tried to obtain reproductions of the most important representations of Berkeley himself. The captions accompanying the photographs will identify the items, and in most cases provide additional commentary. The Introduction outlines his life and work, emphasising his American project. A bibliography is appended. On certain items we have indicated the number assigned to them by Luce in his *Life of Berkeley,* by Kerslake in his *Early Georgian Portraits* (1977), by Foote in *John Smibert Painter* (1950) and by Saunders in his 1979 dissertation *John Smibert (1688-1751): Anglo-American Portrait Painter.*

The result is, we hope, a book that those interested in Berkeley may slip from a shelf without the need to forage in libraries or galleries at a future Berkeley anniversary, or, indeed, at anytime when moved to review Images of Berkeley.

The writers wish to acknowledge the contribution and varied assistance of many individuals and organisations. The American Irish Foundation through the special help of Mr. Billy Vincent and Mr. John Brogan provided generous funding. United States Ambassadors Robert Kane and Margaret Heckler offered enthusiastic support. Mr. Ramie Leahy of Dysart helped conceive the idea. Mr. Brendan J. Dempsey, of Trinity College, was photographic coordinator for the exhibition at the National Gallery of Ireland and for the illustrations in this volume. His work was always professional and his patience and good will much appreciated. Mr. Homan Potterton generously provided the support of the National Gallery. Mr. Raymond Keaveney, of the Gallery, gave vital encouragement to the project. Professor Anne Crookshank, Dr. Patrick Kelly of Trinity College and Mr. John Kerslake read the manuscript and offered many helpful suggestions. Mrs. Jill Berman read the penultimate draft and assured us that there was much to do. Mrs. Rhoda O'Conchúir typed the manuscript and was generally helpful. Professor William Lyons assisted with the proofs. Mrs. Linda Montgomery, Miss Theresa Mulroy, Miss Alva MacSherry, Miss Anne Burke also helped in the preparation of the manuscript.

R.W.H.

Biographical Introduction

George Berkeley, Ireland's greatest philosopher, was born at Kilkenny on 12 March 1685. His early years were spent at Dysart Castle, near Thomastown. After attending Kilkenny College he entered Trinity College, Dublin, in 1700, graduating in 1704. Elected to fellowship in 1707, he was ordained into the Church of Ireland in 1710. By this time he had developed his immaterialist philosophy, which he published in *The Principles of Human Knowledge* (1710), his chief work, and in the more popular *Three Dialogues between Hylas and Philonous* (1713).

Although Berkeley's connection with Trinity College lasted officially until 1724, when he was appointed Dean of Derry, most of his time from 1713 to 1724 was spent away from Ireland. He wrote in England for the *Guardian* (1713) and became friendly with Swift, Pope, Steele and Addison. He travelled extensively in France and Italy. By all accounts, he was a most engaging personality. Bishop Atterbury said of him: "So much understanding, so much knowledge, so much innocence, and such humility, I did not think had been the portion of any but angels till I saw this gentleman". Berkeley was also an acute observer and intrepid traveller; his first-hand account of an eruption of Mount Vesuvius was published in the *Philosophical Transactions* of 1717.

By 1722, however, he had turned his attention from the Old to the New World and boldly determined to establish a college in Bermuda. The college, as he explained in his *Proposal* (1724), was to educate the American colonists and train Indian missionaries to their own people. During the next decade his charm and courage were amply demonstrated by the wide backing he gained for his project. Swift wrote warmly on his behalf. He received large private subscriptions. He obtained a Royal charter and was promised £20,000 by the British Government. In 1729, newly married, he set sail for Rhode Island, which was to be a base for his projected St. Paul's College. Here he lived for nearly three years, waiting in vain for the promised grant. Berkeley was not, however, inactive. He bought a farm and a house in Newport. He preached regularly; he formed friendships with leading American clerics, notably Samuel Johnson; he wrote his major theological work. His interest in American higher education is shown in the gifts of property and books he left to Yale and Harvard.

In late 1731 he returned to London, having been informed that the promised money would never be paid. His second main period of authorship began with *Alciphron: An Apology for the Christian Religion* (1732) — which he composed in Rhode Island — followed by the *Theory of Vision Vindicated* (1733), *The Analyst* (1734), and *A Defence of Free-Thinking in Mathematics* (1735). After two years in England he was appointed to the bishopric of Cloyne, a town twenty miles from Cork, where he spent the next seventeen years. In 1735-7 he published his *Querist*. Composed of nearly a thousand questions, its economic and social suggestions won him the esteem of Irish nationalists. From the *goods* of the mind and fortune, the Bishop next turned to the goods of the body. In *Siris: a Chain of Philosophical Reflexions* (1744), his most enigmatic work, he championed the drinking of tar-water, a medicine of which he learned from America and to which he ascribed great curative powers. His concern for the well-being of all Ireland is evident in his *Word to the Wise, or an Exhortation to the Roman Catholic Clergy of Ireland* (1749), which opens: "Be not startled, Reverend Sirs, to find yourselves addressed by one of a different Communion. We are indeed (to our shame be it spoken) more inclined to hate for those articles wherein we differ, than to love one another for those wherein we agree". In late 1752 Berkeley left Cloyne to supervise his son's education in Oxford. There on 14 January 1752, "this great and good man" — as Berkeley was then described — died "peacefully, indeed happily". He was buried in the Chapel of Christ Church, Oxford.

Berkeley's fame rests chiefly on his philosophy, a philosophy that entitles him to be ranked with Aristotle, Descartes and Hegel. Its central doctrine is that matter does not exist; hence the name *immaterialism*. To many

this has seemed outrageous. Even at Berkeley's own University in Dublin, a commemorative inscription reads: "When the multitude heard, they were astonished at his doctrine". Yet what is matter? If it is what we see and touch, then Berkeley does not deny it. But what do we see and touch, one may ask, if not material things? Berkeley's answer is that we perceive only sensible qualities or ideas: "By sight I have the ideas of light and colours. . . . By touch I perceive . . . hard and soft, heat and cold, motion and resistance. . . . Smelling furnishes me with odours; the palate with tastes, and hearing conveys sounds to the mind". The existence of a physical thing consists in its being perceived: "*esse is percipi*".

Immaterialism provided Berkeley with some of his most impressive arguments for religion. By eliminating matter he hoped to remove the barrier between man and God, thereby inspiring his readers with the presence of God. His philosophy, taken as a whole, constitutes one of the last creative theological syntheses. Its most original insights are employed in the interests of religion. So his *Essay towards a New Theory of Vision* (1709), a landmark in the history of psychology, culminates in an argument that visual data constitute the universal language of God.

"You think he is building a house", observed A. A. Luce, "you find he has built a church". Berkeley's philosophical church is supported not only by his immaterialism and psychology of vision, but also by his searching critique of mathematics and science — in the *Analyst* — which has been called "the most spectacular mathematical event in the eighteenth century in England". His precocious contributions in linguistics, too, were developed in the service of religion. He was probably the first philosopher to see that some words may be significant, even though they do not inform. So words like "hurray", and "gosh", may be meaningful because they evoke emotions, moods and actions. "May we not," he asks, "be affected with the promise of a *good thing,* though we have not an idea of what it is?" He used this insight (now called the emotive theory of language) to defend Christian mysteries.

Yet Berkeley's relevance lies not merely in the parts of his philosophy we now find serviceable. In Europe he is seen as the father of modern idealism. In the Soviet Union, following the lead of Lenin, he is praised as an *honest* subjective idealist. In America he is seen as a precursor of pragmatism. In Ireland he is chiefly remembered for his *Querist.*

Like most cultural heroes, Berkeley influences not only by his works, but by his life. Here his failures have been almost as inspiring as his intellectual successes. His courageous attempt to found a missionary college in Bermuda still endears him to many in America. His prophetic "Verses", which inspired the founders of Berkeley, California, are still evocative; the last stanza runs:

Westward the Course of Empire takes its Way
The four first Acts already past,
A fifth shall close the Drama with the Day
Time's noblest offspring is the last.

Berkeley was the first great Irish-American. His project in the New World helped to establish his moral reputation. It gave substance to Pope's extraordinary tribute: "To Berkeley, ev'ry virtue under heav'n".

D.B.

IMAGES
OF
BERKELEY

1. DYSART CASTLE

Near Thomastown, Co. Kilkenny
Photograph, 1985.

LITERATURE: Luce, 1943; Luce, 1949; *Works of Berkeley,* 1950.

GEORGE BERKELEY spent his early years at Dysart Castle close
by the River Nore, two miles from Thomastown, Co.
Kilkenny, on the back road to Inistiogue. Although he grew
up at Dysart he had been born probably in the townland of
Kilcrin, St. Patrick's parish, Kilkenny. At Dysart the Berkeley
house was attached to the Castle itself on the south-west side.
An ancient chapel stood adjacent on the south-east side. Both
are in total ruins; the castle walls themselves are dangerously
cracked and on the verge of collapse.

The tower may well have been the object of Berkeley's
reference in *Alciphron,* dialogue 4, section ix:

Euphranor: It seems, then that you now think the objects of sight
are at a distance from you?

Alciphron: Doubtless I do. Can any one question but yonder
castle is at a great distance?

Euphranor: Tell me, Alciphron, can you discern the doors,
windows, and battlements of that same castle?

Alciphron: I cannot. At this distance it seems only a small round
tower.

Euphranor: But I, who have been at it, know that it is no small
round tower, but a large square building with
battlements and turrets, which it seems you do not
see.

Alciphron: What will you infer from thence?

Euphranor: I would infer that the very object which you strictly
and properly perceive by sight is not that thing which
is several miles distant.

Alciphron: Why so?

Euphranor: Because a little round object is one thing, and a great
square object is another. Is it not?

Alciphron: I cannot deny it.

Euphranor: Tell me, is not the visible appearance alone the proper
object of sight?

Alciphron: It is.

1

2. KILKENNY COLLEGE
Co. Kilkenny.
Engraving, c.1795.
4½″ × 6½″.
ARTIST: G. Holmes.
ENGRAVER: Greig.
COLLECTION: David Berman.
LITERATURE: Luce, 1949; Rand, 1914.

AT THE AGE of ten Berkeley entered Kilkenny College in the City of Kilkenny, *Cill Choinnigh,* the Church of St. Canice. Kilkenny, a Norman place, was fortified with a castle in 1172 occupied by Strongbow himself. The castle, 100 feet over the River Nore, overlooks the College, founded in 1538 by the 8th Earl of Ormond. The school claims many distinguished alumni. Thomas Prior was a class-fellow of Berkeley; Jonathan Swift (see No. 12) and William Congreve had preceded him.

Berkeley entered the school on 17 July 1696. We have no glimpse of his life in school, but we do have the account of his schoolboy adventure at the Cave of Dunmore (see No. 4).

His friendship with Prior was lifelong (see No. 3). He mentioned but one other individual, Langton, later a curate in Co. Meath, unfortunately remembered by Berkeley as ''somewhat silly''.

2

Engraved by J. Greig from an Original Drawing by G. Holmes.   Published Aug.t 1 1811 by J. Walker & 6 in Rosemans Street, London.

THE COLLEGE at Kilkenny.

3. THOMAS PRIOR OF DUBLIN
(1681-1751)
Mezzotint, 1752.
12.3″ × 10″.

ENGRAVER: Spooner.
COLLECTION: National Library of Ireland.
LITERATURE: Clarke, 1951.

This print was taken from the marble bust by J. Van Nost in the Royal Dublin Society.

THOMAS PRIOR was born in Rathdowney, County Laois, in 1681. He was sent to Kilkenny College at the age of 15 where he became the classmate and, in spite of his seniority, friend of George Berkeley, a friendship destined to last a lifetime. Both matriculated at Trinity College, Prior graduating in 1703 and Berkeley a year later. Their correspondence began early and it is through Berkeley's letters to Prior that we know much of his continental travels. By 1723 Prior, established in Dublin as a man of sound business acumen, had taken over management of Berkeley's often tangled financial affairs: his lawsuit over the Deanery of Dromore, the strange legacy of Hester von Homrigh, Swift's 'Vanessa', (see No. 23), and the ensuing funding of Berkeley's Bermuda project. Desmond Clarke, Prior's biographer, termed him Berkeley's *alter ego*. Often he was a "friendly and helpful advisor"; sometime he acted as agent. He was paid for his service in the Vanessa legacy. Always he was Berkeley's "dear and close" friend.

Berkeley was listed in Prior's *A List of Absentees of Ireland* (1729), a publication which was critical of Irishmen, who, while living abroad, drew large sums of capital from Ireland. In the spirit of Prior's patriotic nationalism, the publication was a courageous act, for it "pilloried" his own class and some of his friends, including Berkeley.

Clarke feels assured that while Prior sent a copy of the first edition to Berkeley in America, to which Berkeley replied with thanks, calling it "... very reasonable and useful", Berkeley's name was not contained in that edition. It did not appear until the second edition. Prior devoted over twenty years of his life to the founding and establishment of the Dublin Society, an idealistic institution dedicated to the improvement of agriculture, technology, the arts and education in Ireland. It was a monumental achievement which anticipated the theory of the Land Grant College movement in America.

The only gap in the Prior-Berkeley correspondence occurs between the years 1731 and 1734, and it is difficult to imagine it definitely lost, in that Prior was meticulous in preserving Berkeley's letters.

The exchange began again in January 1734 when Prior was busily preparing for Berkeley's assumption of the Cloyne Bishopric. Berkeley's work in Cloyne was specifically related to Prior's work with the Dublin Society. Berkeley's spinning school was duly reported. He requested advice from Prior and the Society about agriculture. He requested and received seed for his flax project. Prior, together with Dr. Samuel "Premium" Madden, sponsored competitions and awarded prizes for accomplishment in agriculture, the arts and manufacturing.

Prior figured largely in Berkeley's tar-water controversy. He wrote a widely distributed defence of tar-water called *An Authentick Narrative of the Success of Tar-Water,* listing alleged "proven cures" (see No. 57).

He was associated with Lord Chesterfield, Lord Lieutenant of Ireland, who was considered by the standard of the time sympathetic to humane and just administration. Berkeley induced Prior to present a copy of *The Querist* to Chesterfield,

3

Thomas Prior Esq.
Late Secretary to the Dublin Society

noting the advocacy of a National Bank. Apparently Prior visited Berkeley annually in Cloyne. They once made an excursion together to Killarney, described in a letter of Will Colley, warden of Lohort Castle. Prior preceded Berkeley in death by two years.

A bust was commissioned by the now Royal Dublin Society. It was executed by John Van Nost, who himself had been associated with the Society from 1750 and was the "most distinguished sculptor resident in Ireland." A replica of the Society's bust surmounts the memorial to Prior in the south porch of Christ Church Cathedral, Dublin. On the memorial in Latin are the words of his devoted friend Berkeley:

> Sacred to the memory of Thomas Prior, a man deserving if ever there was one, the best regards of his country. . . .

4. THE "MARKET CROSS" STALACTITE PILLAR, and
PLAN OF THE CAVE OF DUNMORE
Co. Kilkenny.
1875.

LITHOGRAPHER: Edward T. Hardman.
Contained in *Proceedings of the Royal Irish Academy,* Vol. 11, Ser. 11, April 1875, No. 2.
LITERATURE: Hardman, 1875; *Works,* 1951.

THE CAVE of Dunmore, near Kilkenny, is part of an extensive limestone system extending for miles beneath the surface of the countryside. Berkeley explored the cave in July 1699 in company of several school friends. What began as a day of sport, an expedition with gun and dogs, left the young Berkeley profoundly impressed and encouraged his lifelong interest in natural phenomena (see No. 11).

It was six years later, probably in December 1705, that he was moved to write his *Description of the Cave of Dunmore* for presentation to a student society in Dublin. The extant three separate drafts of his essay, written during a very busy time in his life, bear witness to the importance he gave to the experience. It was probably his first work to be made public. It refers to crystalisation and petrification; to problems of solar and terrestrial heat; to the physical theories of Descartes and of Woodward; and to the quantitative methods of physical science.

Towards the beginning of the essay Berkeley writes:

Having gone thro this narrow passage we were surprised to find our selves in a very vast and spacious hall, the floor [of] wch as well as the sides & roof is rock, tho' in some places it be cleft into very frightful chasms yet for the most part is pretty level & coherent; the roof is adorned with a multitude of small round pipes as thick as a goose-quill and (if I misremember not) a foot long or therabouts; [from margin, they are made of an almost transparent stone and are easily broken.] From each of them there distills a drop of clear water wch congealing at the bottom forms a round, hard, & white stone, the noise of those falling drops being somewhat augmented by the echo of the cave seems to make an agreeable harmony amidst so profound a silence; the stones (wch I take to be 3 or 4 inches high they all seeming much of a bigness) standing pretty thick in the pavement make it look very odly. Here is likewise an obelisque of a duskish, gray colour & (I think) about 3 or four foot high, the drop wch formed it has ceased so that it receives no farther increment.

Under the care of the Board of Works the cave is now open as a educational amenity.

4

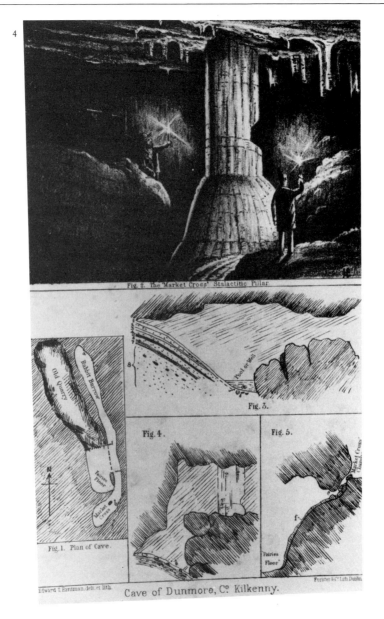

Fig. 2. The 'Market Cross' Stalactitic Pillar.
Old Quarry
Rabbit Burrow
Fairies Floor
Market Cross
N
Fig. 1. Plan of Cave.
Pool or Well
Fig. 3.
Fig. 4.
Fig. 5.
"Fairies Floor"
Edward T. Hardman, del. et lith.
Forster & Co. Lith. Dublin
Cave of Dunmore, Co. Kilkenny.

5. THE RUBRICS

Trinity College, Dublin.
1985.
Oil on Canvas
26″ × 21″.

ARTIST: Ramie Leahy.
COLLECTION: Ramie Leahy.
LITERATURE: Maxwell, 1946.

NONE OF the College buildings which stood during Berkeley's undergraduate years at Trinity remains today, except the row of red brick buildings on the east side of Library Square, and known as the "Rubrics". They are said to date from 1698. The top storey was remodelled in 1894.

6

6. THE PRINTING HOUSE
Trinity College, Dublin.
Photograph, c.1980.
ARCHITECT: Richard Castle.
LITERATURE: Maxwell, 1946.

The Printing House was a gift of the Rev. John Stearne, Bishop of Clogher.

PRIOR TO the erection in 1734 of the Printing House, that ". . . little Doric Temple", printing such as was needed by the University was carried out by tradesmen in the town. Maxwell, in her *History of Trinity College Dublin,* says that ". . . many books were printed [in the Printing House] with their clear type, wide margins and good calf bindings . . . a credit to the University".

The first recorded book was Henry Cope's *Prognostics of Hypocrates* (1736) dedicated to the Lord Lieutenant, Lionel, Duke of Dorset. Although Stearne's gift had included fonts of type, it was Berkeley who gave the first font of Greek type which made possible the publication of the dialogues of Plato in 1738, the first Greek book printed in Ireland.

Richard Castle was a German brought to Ireland by Sir Gustavus Hume.

7. SIR JOHN PERCIVAL

1st Earl of Egmont, (1683-1748).
Mezzotint, c.1725.
15.8″ × 10.3″.
ARTIST: Sir G. Kneller.
ENGRAVER: J. Smith.
LOCATION: National Library of Ireland.
LITERATURE: Rand, 1914; Luce, 1949.

WHILE WE WOULD not wish to diminish the importance of the Berkeley-Prior correspondence, we think that it is the letters between Berkeley and Percival which provide the most significant contribution to our knowledge of Berkeley's life and times. They met probably in the autumn of 1708 and initiated a friendship that lasted forty years. Berkeley dedicated his *Essay on Vision* (1709) to Percival. Percival called Berkeley "A man of the noblest virtues, best learning I ever knew."

Born at Burton, County Cork, on 12 July 1683, Percival was considered particularly as a young man to be a public-spirited landlord, and a person of Irish patriotic nationalism. His later service on the commission dealing with Oglethorp's Georgia scheme seems motivated by a concern for the welfare of the poor and of prisoners in English gaols.

It is through their correspondence that we gauge reaction to Berkeley's early publications. Percival's account of London's response to the *Principles* prompted Berkeley's reply: "Whoever reads my book with due attention will plainly see that there is a direct opposition betwixt the principles contained in it and those of the sceptics, and that I question not the existence of anything that we perceive by our senses."

Berkeley's friendship with Percival helped to provide him with an introduction to London society. In Berkeley's letters to Percival we follow his travels on the continent. Berkeley acquired prints and busts for Percival in Italy. Percival helped Berkeley to procure the deanship at Derry. We know that as a matter of convenience they borrowed money from each other, Berkeley at one time advancing Percival the large sum of £3,000. Percival worked to advance the Bermuda scheme, and attempted to guide Berkeley through the maze of Parliamentary bureaucracy and politics.

We are able to follow the American adventure through their correspondence. Berkeley wrote to Percival providing an account of his visit to Virginia. We have limited descriptions of Newport and his acquisition of Whitehall. In other letters we follow his patient yet anxious wait for the release of parliamentary funding, and finally, Berkeley's discouragement on the abandonment of the scheme.

The friendship continued on Berkeley's return. They met often, and Percival worked for Berkeley's struggle for a bishopric. Berkeley solemnized the marriage of Percival's daughter.

Their correspondence continued until four months before Percival's death in 1748, and thereafter Berkeley maintained a friendship with Percival's son, the second Earl of Egmont.

7

St. John Percivale Bart. of Burton in the County of Cork in Ireland.

8. ARCHBISHOP WILLIAM KING
(1650-1729)

Oil on canvas

40″ × 38″.

ARTIST: Ralph Holland.

LOCATION: Trinity College, Dublin.

LITERATURE: Berman, 1982.

WHEN THE YOUNG Berkeley was writing his philosophical works, Archbishop King was Ireland's most respected philosopher. The Archbishop's reputation then rested on *De Origine Mali* (1702), a book discussed by Leibniz and Bayle, and by Berkeley in the *Philosophical Commentaries*. Of greater interest to Berkeley was King's other major work, *Divine Predestination . . . a Sermon* (1709), which he criticizes in an expansive letter to Sir John Percival, dated 1 March 1709/10, from which we also learn that the 'Appendix' he added to the second edition of the *New Theory of Vision* (1709) was to ''answer the objections of the Archbishop of Dublin.'' In the following month the relationship seems to have reached a crisis when Berkeley was ordained without King's permission by St. George Ashe (Bishop of Clogher and Vice-Chancellor of Trinity College) and was forced to apologize to the Archbishop. His apology is contained in a letter of 18 April 1710, the only one we have between them. Ashe had, apparently, written to King, trying to defend Berkeley's conduct. King tartly replied in a letter of 27 March 1710:

Your Ldp alledges that Mr. Berkly was in a great haste [writes King]. I believe he was as soon as my back was turned, but tho' it be three years as you intimate since he was fellow, yet he never aplyed to me nor I suppose wou'd if I had bin in Dublin, and yet phaps it had not bin the worse for him, if I had discoursed him as I do others before ordination but its plain to avoid that, he desired to be ordained by another, a reason that I think your Ldp shou'd consider well before you approve it. . . .

This passage suggests that King's attitude towards Berkeley was by no means friendly.

9

9. THIRD VIGNETTE

From the Amsterdam Printing (1750) of Berkeley's
Dialogues entre Hylas et Philonous, p. 175.
Engraving, 1750.
1⁷/₁₆″ × 2⁷/₁₆″.

ENGRAVER: Unknown.

COLLECTION: Trinity College, Dublin.

LITERATURE: Berman and Berman, 1982.

THE ENGRAVING illustrates the concluding passage of the *Three Dialogues* (1713), a passage which symbolizes the movement of thought from skepticism to the common sense of immaterialism:

> You see, Hylas, the water of yonder fountain, how it is forced upwards, in a round column, to a certain height; at which it breaks and falls back into the basin from whence it rose: its ascent as well as descent, proceeding from the same uniform law or principle of *gravitation*. Just so, the same principles which at first view lead to *scepticism*, pursued to a certain point, bring men back to common sense.

10. **YOUNG GEORGE BERKELEY**

Oil on canvas, c.1720.

28″ × 22″.

ARTIST: John Smibert.
Luce No. 1, Kerslake No. 56, Foote 1, Saunders 31.
COLLECTION: Mrs. Maurice Berkeley, England.
LITERATURE: Luce, 1949; Foote, 1950; Kerslake, 1977; Saunders, 1979.

THIS IS THE earliest known portrait of Berkeley, painted probably while he was on his second visit to Italy as travelling-companion to George Ashe, the son of Ashe, the Bishop of Clogher. It was on this trip that Berkeley described the rigours of crossing the Alps in winter.

Family tradition indicated that the portrait, which hung in Hanwell Castle for many years, was painted in Rome. Berkeley and Smibert were known to have met in Italy: Smibert, a native of Edinburgh, arrived in Italy at the end of October 1719, to study portrait painting. Although Berkeley's diaries described his travels in detail, it is only recently that we can date this portrait with reasonable accuracy. The discovery of Smibert's *Notebook* and its subsequent publication in 1969 by the Massachusetts Historical Society, provided a clue as to when they met. In his account of his Italian travels, Smibert records that he ". . . received of mr. Ashe in august, 9 bieds of fine Engs. Cloth for a suit of cloths in a present I having given him his head which I had painted". He goes on to report that he "Parted Florance for Rome the 5 of November". Since Berkeley was Ashe's companion or tutor, it seems plausible that he and Smibert were acquainted at least by that time and that Smibert painted Berkeley in Italy sometime late in the summer of 1720. Ashe died at Brussels in 1721.

After Smibert established residence in London in 1722, where in 1725 he moved to Covent Garden, Berkeley often stayed with him. They would later (1728) travel together to America.

10

11. ERUPTION OF MOUNT VESUVIUS

Engraving
From *The Gentleman's Magazine* 1750.
COLLECTION: Trinity College, Dublin.
LITERATURE: Luce, 1949; *Works,* 1951.

DURING HIS travels in Italy in 1717 Berkeley witnessed the eruption of Vesuvius. He described this in a paper for the *Transactions* of the Royal Society.

Berkeley journeyed to Italy twice. His first visit lasted from October 1713 to August 1714, and a second and longer visit from the Autumn of 1716 until the Autumn of 1720. On his first trip, as Chaplain to Lord Peterborough, he crossed Mount Cenis, the most dangerous part of the Alps, on New Year's Day. Although he reported that: "I have not seen anything that should make me desirous to live out of England or Ireland", he also comments that ". . . if you would know lightsome days warm suns and blue skies, you must come to Italy". His second tour allowed him extended time in Italy. He was there by November 1716 and remained until late in 1720. He visited Naples in March 1717. He described it as:

> . . . this happy part of the world . . . soft and delightful beyond comprehension . . . the sky almost constantly serene and blue, the air tempered to a just warmth by refreshing breezes from the sea.

On 17 April he climbed Vesuvius and watched an eruption:

> With much difficulty I reached the top of Mount Vesuvius, in which I saw a vast aperture full of smoak, which hindered the seeing its depth and figure. I heard within that horrid gulf certain odd sounds, which seemed to proceed from the belly of the mountain; a sort of murmuring, sighing, throbbing, churning, dashing (as it were) of waves, and between whiles a noise, like that of thunder or cannon, which was constantly attended with a clattering, like that of tiles falling from the tops of houses on the streets. Sometimes, as the wind changed, the smoak grew thinner, discovering a very ruddy flame, and the jaws of the pan or crater streaked with red and several shades of yellow. After an hour's stay, the smoak, being moved by the wind, gave us short and partial prospects of the great hollow, in the flat bottom of which I could discern two furnaces almost contiguous; that on the left, seeming about three yards in diameter, glowed with red flame, and threw up red-hot stones with a hideous noise, which, as they fell back, caused the forementioned clattering.

His account was sent to his friend Dr. John Arbuthnot, who communicated it to the Royal Society.

11

A Prospect of MOUNT VESUVIUS with its Irruption in 1630

12. DEAN SWIFT

(1667-1745).

Oil on canvas.

74″ × 62″.

ARTIST: Charles Jervas.
COLLECTION: National Gallery of Ireland.
LITERATURE: Luce, 1949.

ONE WOULD BE hard put to imagine a more intriguing combination than Swift and Berkeley. Swift, eighteen years the elder, had preceded Berkeley at Kilkenny College and at Trinity. By the time Berkeley had arrived in London early in 1713, Swift was a celebrated and powerful figure, soon to be appointed Dean of St. Patrick's.

Luce compares them:

> This friendship was in some ways a unity of opposites. Both were strong men, but Swift was imperious and Berkeley gentle; Swift was born to command, Berkeley to persuade. Swift was passionate, Berkeley equable. Swift was often miserly and a misanthrope; Berkeley was always generous and kindly. Both men were thinkers, but Swift was doomed to think without the aid, control, and comfort of philosophy. Both men were masters of the English tongue, Swift of its force and fire, Berkeley of its grace and light. Neither was of robust health; Swift forced himself into fitness by riding and walking; Berkeley, active, tough, and hardly in his prime, sank into sedentary and valetudinarian age. Swift, his own worst enemy, feared or mocked his greatest earthly happiness, the love of Stella; he resolved "not to be fond of children," and inscribed the raven tress (whatever the words mean) "only a

> woman's hair". Berkeley, happily married, was happy in his home and children, and he writes often beautifully, and always sincerely, of "the comforts of domestic life, that natural refuge from solitude and years."

and yet:

> They attended the same school, and graduated from the same university. Both were Irish patriots of English extraction. Both at heart were rebels against the indefensible political system in which their lives were cast, the older man trying to end it, the younger trying to mend it, or at least to alleviate its attendant miseries. Both were Loyal Churchmen; both attacked free-thinking. Both were political economists, and friends of the same poets and essayists. Both are still great names, and if Swift has the greater fame, Berkeley is the greater living influence. Each is mentioned in the other's letters, and we know that they corresponded, but not a letter of the one to the other is known to survive, and we have therefore little or no direct evidence of their feelings for each other.

Although there is no direct evidence of their being together prior to the London period, almost certainly they had met earlier in Dublin. There is some indication that Swift had read Berkeley's *Essay on Vision* and had used the notion of relativity of size in *Gulliver's Travels* (1726).

Even the reserved Luce is moved to a rare exclamation by the thought of Berkeley, Swift and Addison breakfasting together, with Steele joining them: "What a constellation!"

Each served the other well. Swift introduced Berkeley to London society:

12

I went to Court to-day on purpose to present Mr. Berkeley, one of your [?our] Fellows of Dublin College to Lord Berkeley of Stratton. That Mr. Berkeley is a very ingenious man and a great philosopher, and I have mentioned him to all the ministers, and given them some of his writings, and I will favour him as much as I can. This, I think, I am bound to, in honour and conscience, to use all my little credit towards helping forward men of worth in the world.

Later Swift backed Berkeley in the Bermuda enterprise, writing the well-known letter in support of his friend:

There is a gentleman of this kingdom just gone for England; it is Dr. George Berkeley, dean of Derry, the best preferment among us, being worth about £1,100 a year. . . . He is an absolute philosopher with regard to money, titles, and power; and for three years past hath been struck with a notion of founding an university at Bermuda, by a charter from the Crown.

Luce feels that Berkeley's tactful behaviour at the time of the Vanessa affair may have prevented the wrecking of Swift's life. While they corresponded frequently, it is indeed unfortunate that none of the letters is extant. Luce finds no diminution of their regard for each other, their friendship lasting through the ''clouding of Swift's faculties and his general loss of health.''

13. ROBERT, VISCOUNT MOLESWORTH
(1656-1725).
Engraving, 1721.
ARTIST: T. Gibson.
ENGRAVER: P. Pelham.
COLLECTION: National Library of Ireland.
LITERATURE: Berman, 1986.

MOLESWORTH was a friend of Lord Shaftesbury and a patron of John Toland, both targets of Berkeley's *Alciphron*. He was also at the centre of the Dublin intellectual group called the "Molesworth Circle". It was probably Molesworth who was responsible for Berkeley's failure to obtain the living of St. Paul's, Dublin, in 1716.

14

14. GEORGE BERKELEY

with Cumberland Cap.
Oil on canvas, c.1727.
28″ × 25″.
ARTIST: John Smibert?
Not in Luce.
Kerslake No. 57.
LOCATION: Unknown.
LITERATURE: Kerslake, 1977.

JOHN KERSLAKE suggests that this portrait may be the Doctor Berkeley mentioned in Smibert's *Notebook* (p. 84). The portrait sold at Sotheby's, 2nd November 1960, Lot 70. It was formerly in the collection of Lt. Col. Giles Vandeleur, and then acquired by Zeitlin and Ver Brugge, Los Angeles. The face, though younger, is close to that in the painting in the National Portrait Gallery (No. 20), and the chair is similar.

15. **PROPOSAL**
Title-Page.

LOCATION: Trinity College, Dublin.
LITERATURE: Luce, 1949; Keynes, 1976; Gaustad, 1979.

IN THIS PAMPHLET Berkeley sets out his plan for the college in Bermuda. The scheme had been in his mind since 1722, and is outlined in a letter to Percival of 4 March 1722/3·

It is now about ten months since I have determined with myself to spend the residue of my days in the Island of Bermuda, where I trust in Providence I may be the mean instrument of doing good to mankind. Your Lordship is not to be told that the reformation of manners among the English in our western plantations, and the propagation of the Gospel among the American savages, are two points of high moment. The natural way of doing this is by founding a college or seminary in some convenient part of the West Indies, where the English youth of our plantations may be educated in such sort as to supply the churches with pastors of good morals and good learning, a thing (God knows!) much wanted. In the same seminary a number of young American savages may be also educated till they have taken their degree of Master of Arts. And being by that time well instructed in Christian religion, practical mathematics, and other liberal arts and sciences, and early endued with public spirited principles and inclinations, they may become the fittest missionaries for spreading religion, morality, and civil life, among their countrymen, who can entertain no suspicion or jealousy of men of their own blood and language, as they might do of English missionaries . . . I do think the small group of Bermuda Islands the fittest spot for a college on the following accounts. 1. It is the most equidistant part of our plantations from all the rest, whether in the continent, or the isles.

2. It is the only Plantation that holds a general commerce and correspondence with all the rest, there being sixty cedar ships belonging to the Bermudians, which they employ as carriers to all parts of the English West Indies . . . 3. The climate is by far the healthiest and most serene, and consequently the most fit for study. 4. There is the greatest abundance of all the necessary provisions for life, which is much to be considered in a place of education. 5. It is the securest spot in the universe, being environed round with rocks all but one narrow entrance, guarded by seven forts, which render it inaccessible not only to pirates but to the united force of France and Spain. 6. The inhabitants have the greatest simplicity of manners, more innocence, honesty, and good nature, than any of our other planters, who are many of them descended from whores, vagabonds, and transported criminals, none of which ever settled in Bermudas. 7. The Islands of Bermuda produce no one enriching commodity, neither sugar, tobacco, indigo, or the like, which may tempt men from their studies to turn traders, as the parsons do too often elsewhere.

In a key passage in the *Proposal* Berkeley writes:

. . . to any Man [he writes] who considers the divine Power of Religion, the innate Force of Reason and Virtue, and the mighty Effects often wrought by the constant regular Operation even of a weak and small Cause; it will seem natural and reasonable to suppose, that Rivulets perpetually issuing forth from a Fountain or Reservoir of Learning and Religion, and streaming through all Parts of *America,* must in due time have a great Effect, in purging away the ill Manners and Irreligion of our Colonies, as well as the Blindness and Barbarity of the Nations round them: Especially if the Reservoir be in a clean and private Place, where its Waters, out of the way of anything that may corrupt them, remain clear and pure; otherwise they are most likely to pollute than purify the Places through which they flow.

A
P R O P O S A L

For the better Supplying of

C H U R C H E S

IN OUR

Foreign Plantations,

AND FOR

Converting the Savage *Americans* to CHRISTIANITY,

By a COLLEGE to be erected in the *Summer Iflands,* otherwife called the Ifles of *Bermuda.*

The harveft is truly great, but the labourers are few. Luke c. 10. v. 2.

L O N D O N,

Printed by H. WOODFALL, at *Elzevir's-Head,* without *Temple-Bar.* 1725.

Eng⁴ on Steel
THE CITY OF DERRY IN 1686
TAKEN BY PERMISSION FROM THE ORIGINAL PICTURE 1844

16. DERRY IN 1686

Engraving
4.2″ × 6.5″.

LOCATION: National Library of Ireland..
LITERATURE: Luce, 1949; *Works*, 1956.

BERKELEY WAS consecrated Dean of Derry in 1724. In a letter to Percival of 5 May 1724 Berkeley wrote that the Deanery of Derry was a matter of prestige, rather than of money. It was worth £1,500 a year, which sum was offset by charges.

> But as I do not consider it with an eye to enriching myself, so I shall be perfectly contented if it facilitates and recommends my scheme of Bermuda, which I am in hopes will meet with a better reception when it comes from one possessed of so great a Deanery.

He farmed out the tithe lands for £1,250. He was impressed with the city of Derry, and in a letter to Percival of 8 June 1724 he mentions its famous walls, which had in his childhood held back the forces of King James II:

> The city of Londonderry is the most compact, regular, well built town, that I have seen in the King's Dominions, the town house (no mean structure) stands in the midst of a square piazza from which there are four principal streets leading to as many gates. It is a walled town, and has walks all round on the walls planted with trees, as in Padua.

Berkeley never returned to Derry.

17. DERRY FACE COMMEMORATING BERKELEY

LITERATURE: *Works,* 1956.

17

THIS 19th century carved face is one of the corbels on the roof of the nave of St. Columb's Cathedral, Derry, which Berkeley had called "... the prettiest Cathedral in Ireland". In a letter to Percival of 8 May 1724 he wrote:

> My house is a fashionable thing, not five years old, and cost eleven hundred pounds. The Corporation are all good churchmen, a civil people, and throughout English, being a colony from London. I have hardly seen a more agreeable situation, the town standing on a peninsula in the midst of a fine spreading lake, environed with green hills, and at a distance the noble ridge of Ennishawen mountains and the mighty rocks of Maghilligan form a most august scene.

VERSES

ON THE

Prospect of planting ARTS and
LEARNING in *America*.

THE Muse, disgusted at an Age and Clime,
    Barren of every glorious Theme,
In distant Lands now waits a better Time,
    Producing Subjects worthy Fame :

In happy Climes, where from the genial Sun
    And virgin Earth such Scenes ensue,
The Force of Art by Nature seems outdone,
    And fancied Beauties by the true :

In happy Climes the Seat of Innocence,
    Where Nature guides and Virtue rules,
Where Men shall not impose for Truth and Sense,
    The Pedantry of Courts and Schools :

There shall be sung another golden Age,
    The rise of Empire and of Arts,
The Good and Great inspiring epic Rage,
    The wisest Heads and noblest Hearts.

                   Not

Not such as *Europe* breeds in her decay ;
    Such as she bred when fresh and young,
When heav'nly Flame did animate her Clay,
    By future Poets shall be sung.

Westward the Course of Empire takes its Way ;
    The four first Acts already past,
A fifth shall close the Drama with the Day ;
    Time's noblest Offspring is the last.

18

---

18. VERSES

By the Author ON THE Prospect of planting ARTS
and LEARNING in America.

From pages 186-187 of the *Miscellany,* 1752.
LOCATION: Trinity College, Dublin.
LITERATURE: Rand, 1914; *Works,* 1956; Tuveson, 1968; Berman,
1980.

THIS IS THE final version of Berkeley's most famous poem,
published in his *Miscellany* of 1752. An earlier draft had been
sent to Percival on 10 February 1726.

On 7 January 1725 Berkeley was elected to membership in
the Society for the Promotion of Christian Knowledge.
Convinced of the decadence of Europe, in this poem he looked
to the West. In the draft which he finished on 10 February
1726 and sent to Percival, he included the disclaimer:
". . . wrote by a friend of mine with a view to the scheme".
He asked that it be shown to no one outside the family.

The "four first acts" in the last stanza alludes either to the
four ancient kingdoms in the Book of Daniel, or the four phases
in the spread of Christianity.

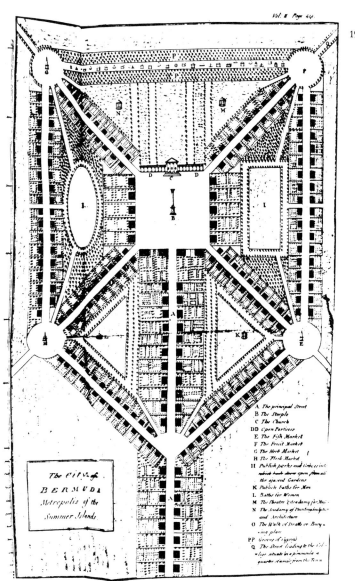

19. PLAN FOR "THE CITY OF BERMUDA METROPOLIS OF THE SUMMER ISLANDS"

Engraving in first collected edition of Berkeley's *Works,* 1784, Vol. II, p. 419.

LOCATION: Trinity College, Dublin.

LITERATURE: Berman, 1977.

THIS PLAN FOR the City of Bermuda was one of at least two Berkeley drew of an ideal community. There originally was a second plan of St. Paul's College, which was to be on a peninsula one quarter of a mile from the city proper. This surviving plan indicates the road to the College.

In her annotated copy of Stock's *Account of Berkeley* (1776), Mrs. Anne Berkeley described the plans from memory. The College was to be, she recalled, in the centre with fellows' houses arranged around it in concentric circles. Her memory seems to have been faulty, however, for Berkeley's plan (illustrated here) shows that the college itself lay at some distance from the city.

20. DEAN BERKELEY POINTING

c.1728.

Oil on canvas.

39½″ × 29½″.

ARTIST: John Smibert.

Luce No. 2; Kerslake No. 62; Foote No. 2; Saunders No. 55; Smibert No. 115.

LOCATION: National Portrait Gallery, London.

LITERATURE: Luce, 1949; Smibert, 1969; Kerslake, 1977; Saunders, 1979; Berman and Berman, 1982.

Gift of Rev. Prebendary William Josiah Irons, DD, 1882.

BERKELEY IS pointing to a rocky island, probably signifying the island of Bermuda, and hence the project. On the island there appears to be running water, a symbolic motif which Berkeley first introduces in the *Proposal* (see No. 15).

The dating of this portrait and its replica or copy is problematic. Two dates have been offered. In 1840 Winter identified the date as 1725, but that date is called into question by the fact that he apparently altered the numbering on the canvas. He describes the situation in a letter quoted by Luce:

> On the right side of the picture immediately over the hand supported by a book is written 'John Smibert 1725'.
>
> The writing is not however as strong and conspicuous as German text and requires a strong light nearly approaching to sun shine to be readily made out. Heckford who lined and cleaned it overlooked the name of the Painter and unluckily rendered the letters still fainter and the two last figures of the date actually rubbed out; so that when it was returned back [sic.] I was obliged

to restore them (see the 25 with my pen, as by a strong light you will perceive).

Luce then says the proper date of 1728 was restored with a cleaning of the painting in 1895, and that he (Luce) prefers the late date, reminding us that Berkeley ''. . . went to lodge with Smibert in August 1725''.

Kerslake dates the portrait 1730 and the copy or replica 1732. The symbolism of the flowing waters, however, would seem to favour an earlier dating, since the *distant* island suggests that the project was at an earlier stage than at the Bermuda group depiction (see below Nos. 26 and 27), where the waters appear to be a good deal closer.

The other version of this portrait is reproduced in Kerslake, 1977.

20

21. DEAN BERKELEY

c.1729.

Oil on canvas.

30″ × 25″.

ARTIST: John Smibert.
Luce No. 3; Foote No. 3; Smibert No. 37.
LOCATION: Massachusetts Historical Society.
LITERATURE: Luce, 1949; Foote, 1950; Smibert, 1969.

LUCE DATES this portrait 1728, and suggests it was painted ". . . on the voyage to America".

Foote more reasonably dates it 1729 and attributes it to the period of Smibert's "residence in Newport". Of course, according to the *Notebook,* Smibert was in Newport for perhaps only three months, but undoubtedly he could have painted it during that time.

21

22

22. BISHOP BERKELEY
After Smibert
Oil on canvas.
42″ × 52″.

ARTIST: Henry Cheevers Pratt 1803-1880.
Mentioned in Luce, No. 4.
COLLECTION: Houghton, Lapan, McKenna.
LITERATURE: Luce, 1949.

THE PRATT portrait of George Berkeley was painted after No. 21. Presented as a gift to Brown University in the mid-nineteenth century, it hung for many years in the University's Sayles Hall. In 1981 three members of the International Berkeley Society acquired the painting to prevent its removal from Rhode Island.

23. A PRESUMED PORTRAIT OF HESTER VAN HOMRIGH ('VANESSA')

Benefactor to Berkeley.

Oil on canvas.

76″ × 63″.

ARTIST: Philip Hussey.
LOCATION: National Gallery of Ireland.
LITERATURE: Luce, 1949.

HESTER VAN HOMRIGH, 1691-1723, the Vanessa in Swift's intended private poem, *Cadenus and Vanessa,* was the daughter of a former Lord Mayor of Dublin. She lived with her parents in London where Berkeley may have encountered her during a visit to the Van Homrigh's home in attendance with Swift. Berkeley was to call her ''a lady to whom I was a perfect stranger, having never in the whole course of my life, to my knowledge, exchanged one single word with her.''

Swift had met her when she was 17 years old. It seems that he had a fatherly interest in her. Vanessa, however, fell in love with him and after inheriting a house in Celbridge, pursued him to Dublin. She wrote him letters of a passionate nature. Suspecting Swift of being married to Stella, Vanessa wrote to Swift demanding to know the truth. Swift, in a fury, confronted her in Celbridge, threw the letter on the table and departed. Vanessa died soon afterwards.

Berkeley was named in her will as recipient of a legacy, which he described as a ''providential event'' and the mark of divine approval and encouragement for the Bermuda scheme. The strange event apparently did nothing to estrange Swift and Berkeley, and indeed Berkeley's discreet handling of the situation as co-executor of the will possibly strengthened their friendship.

24

24. BISHOP CLAYTON AND HIS WIFE

Oil on canvas.
50″ × 69″.
ARTIST: James Latham (1696-1747)
LOCATION: National Gallery of Ireland.
LITERATURE: Berman, 1971; Berman, 1978.

ROBERT CLAYTON was Berkeley's principal assistant in the Bermuda project. In 1737 he introduced Berkeley into the Irish House of Lords.

In his *Principles of the Roman Catholics* (1756) Charles O'Conor links the two men. Reflecting on how the evil of religious conflict in Ireland might be cured, O'Conor writes that it must

". . . be the work of a long time; and I think, it must proceed particularly from the virtue and superior talents of individuals, from some rare spirits, who, like a BERKELEY, or a CLAYTON, take the lead in human knowledge; and who, had they the direction of human affairs, would make the world vastly more wise, and consequently more happy, than hitherto it hath been known to be''.

In 1750 Clayton issued an *Essay on Spirit,* which contains reflections on Berkeley's philosophy. Berkeley criticized the *Essay* in a letter of 7 May 1752: ''. . . the weakness and presumption of the book . . . render it undeserving of any serious answer''.

25. **SEAL OF ST. PAUL'S COLLEGE**
Bermuda.
3¹/₁₆″ diameter.
COLLECTION: Bermuda Historical Society.

25

WHEN BERKELEY left England for the New World, he apparently brought with him the seal for the proposed St. Paul's College, Bermuda. The seal is now owned by the Bermuda Historical Society, a gift from J. C. Hand, who, it is said, acquired it in Jamaica. The intended site of the college in Devonshire parish is now occupied by an Asylum. Berkeley's name is preserved in Bermuda through the Berkeley Institute, a secondary school in Pembroke.

26. DEAN BERKELEY AND HIS ENTOURAGE

The Bermuda Group (Dublin).
Oil on canvas, 1730?
25″ × 30″.
ARTIST: John Smibert.
Mentioned in Luce No. 4; Foote pp. 133-134; Saunders No. 100.
LOCATION: National Gallery of Ireland.
LITERATURE: See 27.
Purchased 1879 by The National Gallery of Ireland from T. Mossop.

27. THE BERMUDA GROUP (YALE)

Oil on canvas, 1739?.
5′ 9½″ × 7′ 9″.
ARTIST: John Smibert.
Luce No. 4; Foote pp. 131-133; Kerslake No. 58.
LOCATION: Yale University Art Gallery, New Haven.
LITERATURE: Luce, 1949; Foote, 1950; Brayton, 1954; Smibert, 1969; Saunders, 1979; Berman and Berman, 1982.
Gift of Isaac Lothrop of Plymouth, Massachusetts.

THERE ARE TWO paintings of the ''Bermuda Group''. While nearly indistinguishable to the casual viewer, there are many obvious as well as subtle differences. The National Gallery painting is the smaller of the two, approximately 2 × 2½ feet; the larger, and we believe later version at Yale, is nearly 6 × 8 feet.

The smaller painting features full length figures of Berkeley himself and of the man seated to the left, who is probably John Wainwright. The Transylvania carpet tablecover is shown in full. There is much detail in this picture, although there is a quick and almost casual immediacy to it. The subtle differences are in the use of colour, particularly in the colour of Dalton's coat, in the position of Miss Handcock's hand, and in the finished details.

While most scholars call this picture either a sketch for the large portrait or a copy or replica of it, it is now virtually certain that it is a sketch and probably dates from late 1729 to sometime in November 1730.

For a full discussion, see No. 27.

THIS SPECTACULAR canvas by John Smibert, America's pioneer portrait painter, portrays the group associated with Berkeley's Bermuda plan. It is called by Foote:

> . . . a tour de force such as the colonies had not seen before. It remained on exhibition in [Smibert's Boston] studio during his lifetime and for many years after his death. . . . It is by far the most interesting and important picture of his entire career and shows the high-water mark of his artistic ability. It set a new standard for colonial painting and is a valuable historical document on account of the individuals represented.

The individuals portrayed are from right to left Berkeley himself; Mrs. Anne Berkeley holding the Berkeley's first child, Henry; Miss Handcock, perhaps daughter of William Handcock, and apparently travelling companion to Mrs. Berkeley. Behind the two women is John James of Bury St. Edmunds, who later succeeded to the baronetcy and returned to England. The seated figure opposite Berkeley is probably John Wainwright, Berkeley's friend and patron, later Baron of the Exchequer in Dublin, who never went to America. For

many years it was believed that Dr. Thomas Moffat, Smibert's nephew, was the seventh figure in the portrait. Smibert's *Notebook* listing, together with the comparison of a mezzotint of Wainwright in Dublin, would seem to confirm the Wainwright identity. To confuse the situation more, the seated figure was previously thought to be John James, now identified as the man standing behind the man seated. Behind Wainwright is Richard Dalton of Lincolnshire, who was to remain in America. In the background is Smibert himself, retiring and unobtrusive. He had met Berkeley in Italy, probably in 1720. They met again in London and Berkeley often stayed with him at Covent Garden (see No. 10). Smibert apparently was to teach art and architecture at the Bermuda college.

There has been considerable discussion of the dating of Nos. 26 and 27. The 1969 publication of *The Notebook of John Smibert* should have cleared up any controversy. It has not.

Entry number 170 in the London *Notebook* lists for July 1728:

A large picture begun for Mr. Wainwright	10-10
	at Boston
10 guineas recd in part	30-30-0

Saunders (pp. 145-6) is convinced this refers to the Bermuda Group; yet as Smibert later painted in Boston a portrait of a Mrs. Wainwright (Smibert No. 32), which *may* have been the large commissioned picture, Saunders' judgement is by no means certain. Entry number 48 in the Boston section of the *Notebook* dated Novr. 1730 lists:

John Wainwright Esqr.
Revd. Dean Berkeley
his Lady and son,
John James Esq.
Ricd. Dalton Esq.
Ms. Hendcock John Smibert

The Yale painting is dated either 1729 or 1739. A recent careful examination of that work is unable to determine whether the third figure (inscribed on the book lying flat on the table) is a 2 or a 3.

The *Notebook* and hence these data were unavailable to Luce, who in 1949 wrote:

Said to have been painted at Boston during the ten days the Berkeleys spent there in September 1731, on the eve of their return to England; long preserved in the Smibert studio, Boston, it was acquired in 1808 by Yale University, where it now hangs in the Trumbull Hall.

Luce, as other scholars, rather dismisses the Dublin painting (No. 26):

A smaller version . . . of the group said to be by Smibert himself was purchased in 1897 for £75 by the National Gallery, Dublin from Mossop of Hampstead.

He does not indicate whether he believes the smaller painting to be a copy or replica of an original or the sketch for it. Foote finds no trouble in simply dating the larger painting. He comments:

Smibert remained with Berkeley in Newport some six months (after May 1729) while the latter was awaiting news that his grant of £20,000 from the Government had become available. In the course of this period he must have executed his large "Bermuda Group" which includes all Berkeley's associates in his proposed enterprise. It is signed and dated Jo. Smibert *fecit* 1729.

Foote also refers casually to No. 26 suggesting it to be ". . . the small copy now in the National Gallery of Ireland in Dublin, or perhaps a study for the original picture. Smibert may well have painted this in Newport before going to Boston". Not having access to the Smibert *Notebook,* Foote does not know that by May 1729 Smibert was in Boston undertaking commissions. The publication of the *Notebook* brought forward the date of his settling in Boston by

. . . six months before he was traditionally reputed to have gone there — within three months of his arrival in America, and long before the hopes of the Bermuda project had faded. So it may be assumed that he went to Boston as an interim measure to make a living by, and to meet the demands for, the services of a competent British artist 'in the most promising field in the Colonies'; a move justified by his having twenty-six sitters in that year (p. 5).

Since James and Dalton did not arrive at Newport with the Berkeleys on 23 January 1729, having proceeded by land from

Virginia, and since Wainwright never arrived at all, it is impossible that between February and May the subjects were together to pose for a portrait. One should also note that at the time Berkeley was busily at work on his house, preaching at Trinity Church and travelling to the Narragansett Country. Even more important, perhaps decisive, is that the boy Henry was not born until June 1729.

It is entirely possible that between June and December 1729 James, Dalton and Smibert came over from Boston. Miss Alice Brayton, in her *Berkeley in Newport,* even suggests that they came to Newport for the baby Henry's christening in September 1729 and that the painting(s) were done to mark the occasion.

It does not seem likely that Smibert, established at a studio in Boston, would transport a large canvas to Newport to complete the work there, especially with his having numerous commissions to finish; nor is there evidence of the portrait's ever having been rolled. It is possible that they all did gather in Newport about the time of the baby's christening in September 1729, and Smibert painted the smaller Bermuda Group as a sketch for the larger. While it is a relatively simple and even rough work the fact is that there is more detail in it than in the larger picture.

To sum up. We know that the larger canvas was dated either 1729 or 1739. We know from Smibert's *Notebook* that *a* Bermuda Group was dated November 1730. We also believe that the smaller painting was a sketch and therefore preceded the larger one. Therefore it seems difficult to resist the conclusion that the smaller canvas (No. 26) must have been finished in 1730 and the larger one (No. 27) in 1739.

28. MISS HANDCOCK POINTING
(Detail of the Yale and Dublin Bermuda Group).
LITERATURE: Berman and Berman, 1982.

I⊤ IS GENERALLY acknowledged that the large Bermuda Group (No. 27) is Smibert's masterpiece, and was recognised as such by the emerging artists living in the colonies. Its fame has been based on the two factors of its brilliant conception and execution, and on the historical importance of the subjects represented.

Beyond these considerations the painting obviously has narrative meaning. Berkeley himself stands presiding over the group; Mrs. Berkeley, the new mother, sits proudly at his side; James is behind her; Wainwright is seated with pen and book; Dalton watches attentively; Smibert lurks knowingly yet deferentially in the background.

The focus of the painting and possibly its message is in the left hand of Mrs. Berkeley's companion, Miss Handcock. In both versions of the portrait her hand is pointing at running water in the background, the graphic expression of Berkeley's water-passage in the *Proposal* (quoted above, No. 15), where Berkeley identifies his college with "a fountain or reservoir of learning and religion".

Perhaps the most significant difference between the two versions, although it has not been generally noticed, is in the positioning of Miss Handcock's left hand. In the Dublin painting (A) she is pointing fairly naturally, with her index finger in an upward position, whereas in the Yale painting (B) her hand, as Foote noticed, is "held rather awkwardly", and, perhaps even more interestingly, the index finger is in a downward and inverted position. If one accepts that Miss Handcock is symbolically pointing to the group's purpose, then one might well be tempted to find meaning in these contrasting hand positions; the one (A) painted when hopes were high, and the other (B) painted after the project had failed and most of the group had returned to the Old World.

If, as is most likely, the large painting was finished by Smibert in 1739, long after the project's failure, the unnatural position of Miss Handcock's hand and downward turning of the index finger might well have been his way of symbolizing that the hopes expressed in the running-water motif had now been dashed.

28

A

B

29

NEWPORT, R.I. IN 1730.

29. NEWPORT
in 1730.

ARTIST: John R. Newell.
Lithograph from an over-mantel painting in the possession of James Philips.
COLLECTION: Newport Historical Society.
LITERATURE: Luce, 1949; *Works,* 1956; James, 1975.

NEWPORT, Rhode Island, was a thriving seaport at the time of Berkeley's arrival in 1729. He was surprised at its prosperity and modernity. It was his plan to use the area as a base for the working out of the Bermunda project.

Newport then exceeded Providence in population and in commercial activity. Newport merchants and ships' captains had built up trade with the Caribbean islands, as well as along the entire North American coast. The General Assembly of the Colony met in Newport from time to time, involving the town in many phases of the Colony's political affairs.

Newport's population was diverse, including wealthy merchants, farmers from the surrounding area, shopkeepers, black and native American slaves. Newport society nurtured its own social élites, a tradition it maintains to this day. The diversity of the economic base of the town was matched by the diversity of religious persuasion represented there, Quakers, Baptists, Congregationalists, Anglicans, Presbyterians, and some, as Berkeley indicated, embracing no religion at all.

Berkeley wrote in a letter to Percival:

> The town of Newport contains about six thousand souls, and is the most thriving flourishing place in all America for its bigness. It is very pretty and pleasantly situated. I was never more agreeably surprised than at the first sight of the town and its harbour.

30. **TRINITY CHURCH,**
Newport, Rhode Island.
Built by Richard Mundy 1726.
Photograph c.1982.
LITERATURE: Mason, 1890; *Works,* 1956; Downing and Scully, 1967.

THEN, AS NOW, Trinity is one of the most beautiful churches in America. Berkeley preached there many times during his stay in Newport.

Trinity Church is the oldest Anglican parish in New England. It has maintained uninterrupted service to its parishioners since its establishment in 1698. The original church, built in 1702, was outgrown by the parish and the existing church was built in 1726 by Newport Master Carpenter Richard Mundy.

During a sermon on 27 April 1729 Berkeley apparently aroused the ire of parishioners when he preached on the superiority of the Church of England. He reacted in a letter to Percival of 30 August 1729:

> For the first three months I resided at Newport and preached regularly every Sunday, and many Quakers and other sectaries heard my sermons in which I treated only those general points agreed by all Christians. But on Whit-Sunday (the occasion being so proper) I could not omit speaking against that spirit of delusion and enthusiasm which misleads those people: and though I did it in the softest manner and with the greatest caution, yet I found it gave some offence, so bigoted are they to their prejudices. Till then they almost took me for one of their own, to which my

everyday dress, being only a strait-bodied black coat without plaits on the sides, or superfluous buttons, did not a little contribute.

Excepting Whitehall, Berkeley's home, Trinity Church is the building most closely associated with him in Rhode Island. He preached from its wine-glass pulpit, the only one of its kind surviving in America. The grave of his infant daughter, Lucia, buried on 5 September 1731, three days before his departure for England, is in the churchyard.

31. REVEREND JAMES HONYMAN

Oil on canvas.
38″ × 49¾″.
ARTIST: G. Gaines.
COLLECTION: Trinity Church, Newport.
LITERATURE: Mason, 1890; *Works,* 1956.

REV. JAMES HONYMAN (1704-1750) was the first Church of England missionary appointed to New England by the Society for the Propagation of the Gospel in Foreign Parts. He was the Rector of Trinity Church in Newport at the time of Berkeley's arrival. In fact, local lore has it that when news of Berkeley's imminent arrival was brought to Honyman he dismissed the congregation and led the parishioners to the dockside to greet the Dean.

The Berkeleys lived with the Honymans from the time of their arrival in Newport until their Rhode Island home, Whitehall, was completed. The tract of land purchased by Berkeley in what is now Middletown, Rhode Island, adjoined the Honyman farm lands. The only recorded marriage performed by Berkeley in America was that of Honyman's daughter Elizabeth to William Mumford on 27 May 1729.

Honyman is recognized as the "Father of the Parish". Under his direction the congregation outgrew the original church building and the present church was constructed. On 28 March 1729 Berkeley wrote of him:

Mr. Honyman, the only Episcopal clergyman in this Island, in whose house I now am, is a person of very good sense and merit on all accounts, much more than I expected to have found in this place.

32

32. WHITEHALL
Middletown, Rhode Island.
Photograph, c.1980.
LITERATURE: Luce, 1949; Downing and Scully, 1967.

WHITEHALL, SITUATED on a ninety-six acre tract of land approximately three miles from Newport, was probably designed and expanded from an existing structure under Berkeley's direction. With the assistance of Daniel Updike, then Attorney General of the Colony, and member of the Vestry of Trinity Church, Berkeley acquired the property from Joseph Whipple.

While Berkeley was in residence Whitehall was a productive farm from which he had intended to supply the college in Bermuda. Whitehall, in addition, became a meeting place for Anglican clergy, a place of tranquillity where Berkeley could undertake and complete his work, *Alciphron,* as well as the site of his intensive philosophical discussions with Samuel Johnson (see No. 35).

Upon his departure from Rhode Island Berkeley gave Whitehall and its lands to Yale with the stipulation that the income from the holdings be used to support three scholars yearly. During the American Revolution Whitehall was used as headquarters by the British.

By the 1890s Whitehall had fallen into serious disrepair. Three Newport women acquired and restored the house. It was then given to the National Society of the Colonial Dames in the State of Rhode Island and Providence Plantations, who very meticulously maintain the house as a Berkeley memorial to this day.

None of Berkeley's furnishings remain; however, the house contains pieces representative of his day. Some early editions of his works are on the book shelves.

33

33. REVEREND GEORGE BERKELEY, D.D.

Oil on canvas.

30″ × 25″.

ARTIST: Alfred Hart.

Mentioned in Luce, 1949.

COLLECTION: Redwood Library and Atheneum, Newport.

34. ENGRAVING OF BERKELEY

With Signature.

ENGRAVER: William Hull.

Frontispiece of Fraser's *Life and Letters,* 1871, taken from the Yale Bermuda Group (No. 27).

COLLECTION: David Berman.

LITERATURE: Berman, 1985 (b).

A. C. FRASER, a Scotsman, was the leading Berkeley scholar of the nineteenth century. He set a precedent not only for high scholarship but also for longevity — in both of which he was followed by Luce, who, like Fraser, lived into his nineties (see Nos. 65 and 66).

34

35. REVEREND SAMUEL JOHNSON
1696-1772.

Oil on canvas, c.1730.

30¹/₁₆″ × 12¾″.

ARTIST: John Smibert.
Smibert No. 139; Saunders No. 155.
COLLECTION: Columbia University in the City of New York.
LITERATURE: Luce, 1949; *Works,* 1956 and 1957; Berman, 1977.
Gift of Mr. Kilbourn, 1756.

GEORGE BERKELEY's friendship with Samuel Johnson is of major significance in the development of American philosophy, American higher education, and in the understanding of Berkeley's thought. Johnson, himself an Anglican clergyman, was well acquainted with Berkeley's works prior to the Dean's arrival in Newport. Introduced by Honyman, Johnson called on Berkeley at Whitehall where they had philosophical conversations of several days' duration. Mrs. Berkeley reports that Johnson was a frequent visitor at Whitehall.

Of particular importance is the Berkeley-Johnson correspondence which came about during Berkeley's Rhode Island residence. Johnson's queries afforded Berkeley the opportunity to respond to philosophical questions which had been of concern to many of his critics.

It was through Johnson's influence that Berkeley left to Yale the books he had brought with him for St. Paul's College. Berkeley shipped additional volumes to Yale on his return to Britain.

Of particular significance for American higher education is a letter written in 1749 from Berkeley to Johnson which provides advice on the organization and operation of King's College, New York. Samuel Johnson became its first president. The college was later renamed Columbia University. The letter is owned by the Columbia University Library.

In dedicating his *Elementa Philosophica* (1752) to Berkeley, Johnson revealed his intellectual debt to him.

36. REVEREND JAMES MacSPARRAN
1693-1757.

Oil on canvas, c.1735.

30″ × 35″.

ARTIST: John Smibert.

Saunders No. 145; Smibert No. 111.

COLLECTION: Bowdoin College Museum of Art, Brunswick, Maine.

LITERATURE: Updike, 1847; Goodwin, 1899; Luce, 1949.

REV. JAMES MacSPARRAN, born in Dungiven, County Derry in 1693, was rector at St. Paul's Church a few miles south of the village of Wickford on the western shore of Narragansett Bay.

Berkeley was introduced to MacSparran probably by Col. Daniel Updike, a prominent West Bay plantation owner. It was in the company of MacSparran that Berkeley made the first of many journeys to the "Narragansett Country" to learn of the conditions of the indigenous population which had not then been incorporated into the slavery system of the colony. Berkeley preached the first of the numerous sermons he was to deliver at St. Paul's on Sunday 11 May 1729.

Berkeley made visits to the Narragansett Country sometimes in the company of the painter, Smibert, and Daniel Updike. It was during these visits that he gathered the material for the address he delivered in February 1732 to the Society for the Propagation of the Gospel in Foreign Parts. Here he decried the miserable plight of the Indians, and called to task the English planters as those responsible for the deterioration of the minds and souls of these people.

Berkeley's visits to the West Bay usually extended over several days to include observations of the native Americans, delivery of a Sunday sermon and enjoyment of the hospitality for which the MacSparran household was well known.

37

37. ST. PAUL'S CHURCH

Wickford, Rhode Island.
Photograph, c.1982.
LITERATURE: Updike, 1847; *Works,* 1956.

WRITING TO Percival, Berkeley notes:

I live now in the country and preach occasionally, sometimes at
Newport, sometimes in the adjacent parts of the continent.

St. Paul's Church, in later years referred to as the ''Old
Narragansett Church'', was built in 1707 at a site known as
the Platform, a few miles south of the village of Wickford.
The Church's rector was James MacSparran (see No. 36).

The famous American portrait painter, Gilbert Stuart, was
baptised by MacSparran in the Church on April 11, 1756. Stuart
himself was later to spend several years in Dublin, where he
painted the portraits of a number of eminent Irish people.

38

38. COCUMSCUSSOC OR SMITH'S CASTLE

Watercolour, c.1980.

14″ × 20″.

ARTIST: W. Spencer Crooks.

COLLECTION: W. Spencer Crooks.

LITERATURE: Updike, 1842 and 1847.

COCUMSCUSSOC, sometimes known as Smith's Castle, is one of the few remaining Rhode Island houses closely associated with Berkeley. Rallying point for the Great Swamp Fight, which was decisive in crushing the indigenous population in 1675, haven for French Huguenots during 1686, Cocumscussoc emerged by the time of Berkeley's visits there as one of the first slave-holding plantations in the Narragansett Country.

Situated on land acquired from Roger Williams, founder of the Colony of Rhode Island, the original structure was burned by Native Americans in 1676. A portion of the existing structure was completed prior to 1691.

Berkeley is reported to have made many visits to Cocumscussoc in the company of Smibert, MacSparran, and his host Col. Daniel Updike.

Daniel Updike met Berkeley early in his stay in Rhode Island. He was a cultivated gentleman, Attorney General of the Colony, who knew Greek, Latin and French. The library at Cocumscussoc included both classical and general literature.

Updike along with Reverend James Honyman, Berkeley's host prior to the completion of Whitehall (No. 31), was one of the founders of the Literary and Philosophical Society which in later years grew into the Redwood Library and Athenaeum. Berkeley is acknowledged as the inspiration for this group, as well as one who gave it direct support.

39

39. GEORGE BERKELEY

Oil on canvas, c.1732.
44½" × 35¾".

ARTIST: John Smibert?
National Gallery of Ireland, No. 895; Luce No. 13 — listed as
doubtful; Saunders No. 110.
COLLECTION: National Gallery of Ireland.
LITERATURE: Luce, 1949; Saunders, 1979.

Luce sees this painting as a composite portrait drawn from
Vanderbank (No. 54) and Smibert (No. 27).

Saunders, however, suggests that the painting has a more
distinguished pedigree:

> A portrait of Dean Berkeley commissioned after he had departed
> for England may possibly be the three-quarter length now in the
> National Gallery of Ireland and previously attributed to an
> anonymous British artist. (p. 153)

Drawn by A. A. Harwood

Hanging Rock near Newport R. I. with a view of Sachuest beach & Purgatory.
Under the alcove of the Hanging Rock Dean Berkley wrote his Minute Philosopher!

40. HANGING ROCK

near Newport, Rhode Island, sometimes called
"Berkeley's Seat", with a View of Sachuset Beach
and Purgatory.
Lithograph.
10″ × 6⅝″.

ARTIST: A. A. Harwood.
COLLECTION: Newport Historical Society.
LITERATURE: Luce, 1949; Brayton, 1954.

IN THE SECOND dialogue of *Alciphron,* Berkeley writes:

> After breakfast, we went down to the beach about a half mile
> off; where we walked on the smooth sand, with the ocean on
> one hand, and on the other, wild, broken rocks, intermixed with
> shady trees and springs of water. . . . We then withdrew into
> a hollow glade between two rocks.

Local lore has it that Berkeley wrote *Alciphron* while seated
in the hollow which Harwood depicts. The spot is a pleasant
walk from Berkeley's home, Whitehall, through country that
in Berkeley's time would have been open fields. The Bishop's
Seat is accessible now by woodland trails which are part of
the Norman Bird Sanctuary.

41. ALCIPHRON FIRST VIGNETTE

Engraving, 1732.

ARTIST: probably Vanderbank.
COLLECTION: Trinity College, Dublin.
LITERATURE: Berman and Berman, 1985.

THIS VIGNETTE AND the next one can be read in two ways. Exoterically, they illustrate the text of *Alciphron,* Berkeley's defence of natural and revealed religion. Esoterically, they refer to his (by then abortive) American project. The key passage from the *Proposal* helps to explain the esoteric meaning of the first vignette. Here Berkeley describes his projected college as a 'Fountain or Reservoir of Learning and Religion' (see No. 15).

By 1732, however, the projected college, the 'Fountain of Learning' had failed; and the first vignette conveys this defeat by the 'Fountain of living waters', which according to the motto from Jeremiah II.13, is 'forsaken' for 'broken cisterns that can hold no water'. Esoterically, the vignette symbolizes the project's abandonment by the English government as well as by Berkeley's associates. Exoterically, it illustrates the rejection of God and religion by the freethinkers or — as Berkeley calls them, following Cicero — minute philosophers, against whom *Alciphron* was written. In dialogue one, section x, Berkeley exploits the vignette's other motto, taken from Cicero's *De Senectute* 85:

> But if when dead I will be without sensation, as some minute philosophers think, then I have no fear that these seers, when they are dead, will have the laugh on me.

41

ALCIPHRON:
OR, THE
MINUTE PHILOSOPHER.
IN
SEVEN DIALOGUES.
Containing an APOLOGY *for the* Christian Religion,
against those who are called Free-thinkers.

VOLUME *the* FIRST.

They have forsaken me the Fountain of living waters, and hewed them out cisterns, broken cisterns that can hold no water. Jerem. ii. 13.
Sin mortuus, ut quidam minuti Philosophi censent, nihil sentiam, non vereor ne hunc errorem meum mortui Philosophi irrideant.
Cicero.

LONDON:
Printed for J. TONSON in the *Strand,* 1732.

Berkeley writes:

. . . the modern Free-thinkers are the very same with those *Cicero* called Minute Philosophers, which name admirably suits them, they being a sort of Sect which diminish all the most valuable Things. . . .

42

42. ALCIPHRON SECOND VIGNETTE
Engraving, 1732.
ARTIST: probably Vanderbank.
COLLECTION: Trinity College, Dublin.
LITERATURE: Berman and Berman, 1985.

EXOTERICALLY AND superficially, the vignette and its mottoes may refer to what Berkeley considers the chameleon character of his free-thinking opponents. But who, more specifically, is the female figure on the pedestal, and why is she stopping her ears with her forefingers? Berkeley's little known and highly fanciful *Guardian* essay of 25 April 1713 shows that she stands for Prejudice. Here 'Ulysses Cosmopolita' (Berkeley) tells how having taken a marvellous 'philosophical snuff' he visited the pineal gland of the author of the irreligious *Discourse of Free-Thinking* (1713), Anthony Collins. The passage runs:

> . . . having left my body locked up safe in my study, I repaired to the Grecian coffee-house, where, entering into the pineal gland of a certain eminent Free-thinker, I made directly to . . . the understanding . . . but . . . found the place narrower than ordinary, insomuch that there was not any room for a miracle, prophesie, or *separate spirit*. . . . I discovered Prejudice in the figure of a woman standing in a corner, with her eyes close shut, and her fore-fingers stuck in her ears; many words in a confused order, but spoken with great emphasis, issued from her mouth.

But what has free-thinking Prejudice to do with the seated figure, or with Berkeley's American scheme? The answer may be found in a letter he wrote on 2 March 1730/1, when forces seemed to be conspiring against his Bermuda project:

> what [is] foolishly called free-thinking seems to me the principal cause or root not only of opposition to our College but most other evils in our age. . . .

So, as the first vignette (No. 41) declares the abandonment of Berkeley's missionary project, the second depicts the force which had defeated it: Freethinking prejudice; and both vignettes identify the target of *Alciphron* — the freethinkers, whose infidelity Berkeley describes as 'an Effect of Narrowness and Prejudice' (in dialogue six, section xi).

The figure seated in the foreground of the vignette would seem to be Robert Walpole. By refusing to pay the £20,000 granted by Parliament he was chiefly responsible for defeating Berkeley's project. While ostensibly supporting the scheme — indeed, he gave it money from his own pocket — he really opposed it. Stock, in his *Account of Berkeley* (1776), relates the final phase of Walpole's dissembling:

> After having received various excuses [about the payment of £20,000 grant] Bishop Gibson, at that time bishop of London (in whose diocese all the West Indies are included) applying to Sir Robert Walpole then at the head of the treasury, was favoured at length with the following very honest answer: 'If you put this question to me' says Sir Robert, 'as a minister, I must and can assure you, that the money shall most undoubtedly be paid as soon as suits with public convenience; but if you ask me as a friend, whether Dean Berkeley should continue in America, expecting the payment of £20,000, I advise him by all means to return home

to Europe, and to give up his present expectations'. The Dean being informed of this conference by his good friend the Bishop, and thereby fully convinced that the bad policy of one great man had rendered abortive a scheme whereon he had expended much of his private fortune, and more than seven years of the prime of his life, returned to Europe.

That the seated figure represents Walpole is supported by the context of the quotation from Hosea, where it is a merchant who is holding the balances of deceit: and given Walpole's position as head of the treasury and his close connection with the City, the parallel is appropriate. Walpole also seems to have been known as a sceptic in religion, so that he is suitably represented as resting on the plinth of irreligious Prejudice, which is blocking the view of the (living) water in the background.

43

43. **WHITE HORSE TAVERN**
Newport, Rhode Island.
Photograph, c.1980.
LITERATURE: Downing and Scully, 1967.

ON THE CORNER of Marlborough and Farewell Streets in Newport stands the White Horse Tavern, the oldest public house in continuous operation in the United States. The building served temporarily as a meeting place for the General Assembly prior to the completion of the Colony House, and as a hostelry for visitors to Newport until the time of its occupation by the British. During Berkeley's residence the White Horse was the political and social centre of Newport.

44. BERKELEY COFFEE POT

Photograph.
Silver.
CRAFTSMAN: Paul Crespin.
LOCATION: Trinity Church, Newport, Rhode Island.
LITERATURE: Updike, 1842.

44

ACCORDING TO Wilkins Updike this silver coffee pot was given to Col. Daniel Updike by Berkeley on his departure from Newport.

> In testimony of the friendship and esteem which the Dean entertained for Mr. Updike, he presented him, on his departure for Europe, an elegantly wrought silver coffee pot, and after his arrival, sent him his 'Minute Philosopher', which now remain in the family, as remembrances of this distinguished divine.

The pot was given to Trinity Church, Newport in 1936 by an Updike descendant.

45

45. TRINITY CHURCH ORGAN

Photograph, c.1981.
Constructed by Richard Bridge, London, 1733.
Trinity Church, Newport, Rhode Island.
LITERATURE: Mason, 1890; *A visit,* 1973.

A TREASURED possession of Trinity Church is the organ Berkeley gave it in 1733. The organ, the second in New England, was built by Richard Bridge of London and approved, it is said, by Handel.

The building of the organ, testing, disassembly for shipment, and reassembly in Newport was a most noteworthy undertaking. Minutes of a Vestry Meeting of Trinity Church 25 February 1733 record that

> . . . the Rev. Mr. Honyman is desired to draw up a letter of thanks to the Rev. Mr. Dean Berkeley, for his generous present of an organ to this Church, and likewise a letter of thanks to Mr. Henry Newman, for his care about and shipping the same; in order to be sent to England as soon as conveniently may be.

They sought to raise subscriptions of £250 to defray the cost of setting up the organ.

When it came to the matter of finding an organist, it was necessary to send to England for Mr. John Owen Jacobi. Such notable Colonial composers as Charles Pachelbel and William Selby are known to have played the instrument.

The original casework remains. Surprisingly, the Royal Crown and Bishop's mitre on the organ-casing survived the American Revolution and remain carefully preserved. The original keyboard is on display at the Newport Historical Society.

46. TITLE-PAGE OF BERKELEY'S PRINCIPLES AND THREE DIALOGUES

1734.

LOCATION: Trinity College, Dublin.
LITERATURE: *Works,* 1949; Keynes, 1976.

THIS IS THE title-page of the last authorized printing of Berkeley's two most famous philosophical works, containing notable revisions of the previous editions of twenty years earlier.

Much of Berkeley's immaterialist thesis is contained in the *Principles,* section 3:

3 That neither our thoughts, nor passions, nor ideas formed by the imagination, exist without the mind, is what every body will allow. And it seems no less evident that the various sensations or ideas imprinted on the sense, however blended or combined together (that is, whatever objects they compose) cannot exist otherwise than in a mind perceiving them. I think an intuitive knowledge may be obtained of this, by any one that shall attend to what is meant by the term *exist* when applied to sensible things. The table I write on, I say, exists, that is, I see and feel it; and if I were out of my study I should say it existed, meaning thereby that if I was in my study I might perceive it, or that some other spirit actually does perceive it. There was an odour, that is, it was smelled; there was a sound, that is to say, it was heard; a colour or figure, and it was perceived by sight or touch. This is all that I can understand by these and the like expressions. For as to what is said of the absolute existence of unthinking things without any relation to their being perceived, that seems perfectly unintelligible. Their *esse* is *percipi,* nor is it possible they should have any existence, out of the minds or thinking things which perceive them.

46

A

TREATISE

Concerning the

PRINCIPLES

O F

HUMAN KNOWLEDGE.

WHEREIN THE

Chief Caufes of Error and Difficulty in the *Sciences,* with the Grounds of *Scepticifm, Atheifm,* and *Irreligion,* are inquired into.

Firft Printed in the Year **1710.**

To which are added

THREE DIALOGUES

BETWEEN

Hylas and *Philonous,*

In Oppofition to

SCEPTICKS *and* ATHEISTS.

Firft Printed in the Year **1713.**

Both written by *GEORGE BERKELEY,* M. A. Fellow of *Trinity-College, Dublin.*

LONDON: Printed for *Jacob Tonfon,* **1734.**

47. GEORGIUS BERKELEY S.T.P.

Oil on canvas, May 1733.

49″ × 39″.

ARTIST: Unknown.

Luce No. 5.

LOCATION: Lambeth Palace, London.

LITERATURE: Kerslake, 1977; Berman and Berman, 1982.

THE SHIP ON the stormy sea is probably meant to symbolise Berkeley's arduous and abortive Bermuda Project. It represents the Bermuda Project in retrospect and effectively marks its end. Through the portraits and frontispieces we are able to see the Project in distant prospect (No. 20), as hopeful actuality (Nos. 26 and 27), as defeated and abandoned (Nos. 41-42, 53-55), and in stormy retrospect (No. 47). The book that Berkeley holds is entitled *Voyage to the Indies.*

Little is known of this portrait. It was at Lambeth Palace by 1781.

48. FRONTISPIECE TO THE FIRST COLLECTED WORKS (1784)

Engraving, 1 Aug. 1781.

8½" × 6¼".

After the Lambeth Palace Portrait (No. 47).

ENGRAVER: T. Cooke.

COLLECTION: David Berman.

THIS IS PROBABLY the most popular engraving of Berkeley.
Many variations of it are to be found in the nineteenth century.

48

49. BERKELEY CASTLE PORTRAIT

Oil on canvas, c.1734.
48″ × 40″.
ARTIST: Unknown.
LOCATION: Berkeley Castle, Gloucestershire.
LITERATURE: Berman, 1978; T.C.D. Manuscript 3530.
Probably given to Lord Berkeley by Eliza Berkeley in her will. Not listed in Luce.

BERKELEY CASTLE has been the historic seat of the Berkeley family since the 11th century. It is mentioned by Shakespeare in *Richard the Second.* When Berkeley became Bishop he impailed the arms of the Berkeley Castle branch with those of Cloyne. In Mrs. Delany's correspondence there is a footnote that describes Berkeley as a cadet of the family of Lord Berkeley. Although this portrait is not included in Luce nor mentioned by Kerslake, in Berkeley Castle it is confidently said to be of Bishop Berkeley.

It was first mentioned by Berman in the *Berkeley Newsletter* 2 (1978). After comparing this portrait with other known likenesses, his conclusion was: "On balance, I am prepared to accept the attribution of those at Berkeley Castle". Since then new evidence has come to light which confirms the attribution. In a hitherto unnoticed will of Eliza Berkeley, now in Trinity College, Dublin, she has the following note, dated 22 November 1797:

In consequence of a letter this day received by me from the Earl of Berkeley, I desire that if I do not live to send it [,] Mr. Grimston will send to *Berkeley Castle* that Portrait of Bishop Berkeley in Lawn Sleeves — mitre &c on the frame now at the house of my Friend Mr. Duncombe. . . .

Round Tower Cloyne

50. ROUND TOWER, CLOYNE

Pencil drawing, c.1840.
9½″ × 7½″.

ARTIST: Henry O'Neil?
COLLECTION: David Berman.
LITERATURE: Luce, 1949; *Works,* 1956; O'Loingsigh, 1977.

THE STYLE OF THE Round Tower of Cloyne suggests that it was built in the eleventh century. It was originally ninety-two feet in height and had the usual conical crown. The Tower was severely damaged by a violent thunder storm on the night of 10 January 1747 during Bishop Berkeley's residence in Cloyne. Berkeley refers to the event in a letter dated 2 February 1749:

Our Round Tower stands where it did, but a little stone arched vault on top was cracked and must be repaired. The bell also was thrown down and broke its way through three boarded stories, but remains entire. The door was shivered into many very small pieces and dispersed; and there was a stone forced out of the wall.

51. **ST. COLMAN'S CATHEDRAL**
Cloyne, County Cork.
Photograph, c.1982.
LITERATURE: Luce, 1949; O'Loingsigh, 1977.

Cloyne cathedral was built in the mid-thirteenth century on the site of more ancient buildings. It is dedicated to St. Colman, the seventh-century bard, saint, and a companion to St. Finbarre of Cork. George Berkeley was bishop here from 1734 until his departure for Oxford in 1752.

52

VIEW OF THE PALACE OF CLOYNE.

From the South or Garden front

52. BISHOP'S PALACE

Cloyne, Co. Cork.

Engraving.

7″ × 10″.

LOCATION: National Library of Ireland.

LITERATURE: Luce, 1949; O'Loingsigh, 1977.

BERKELEY'S HOME from 1734 to 1752. It was from the Palace that he exerted an effective social influence during his bishopric; he instituted technical training programmes, gave assistance to the poor, organized cultural events, and advocated tar-water as a universal medical cure. The original Bishop's Palace was built by John Bird, Bishop of Cloyne, in the fourteenth century. It was reported that in Berkeley's time:

. . . in the Episcopal Palace of Cloyne, the eye was entertained with great variety of good paintings, as well as the ear with concerts of excellent music.

Crofton Croker described the palace as:

. . . an old fashioned and clumsy building without any claims to architectural beauty; but as the residence of the amiable Bishop Berkeley possesses a superior attraction.

53

THE RIGHT REVD   GEORGE BERKELEY, S.T.P.
LATE LORD BISHOP OF   CLOYNE IN IRELAND.

53. **THE RIGHT REVD. GEORGE BERKELEY S.T.P.**

Late Bishop of Cloyne in Ireland.
Engraving.
1800.
10¼″ × 13″.

ARTIST: John Vanderbank.
ENGRAVER: Skelton.
Luce No. 6.
LOCATION: Marsh's Library, Dublin.
LITERATURE: T.C.D. Manuscript No. 3530, f.13; Berman and Berman, 1982.

THE ORIGINAL of this engraving was almost certainly in the possession of Eliza Berkeley, who probably commissioned it, as the same engraver executed an engraving of her son, George Monck Berkeley, for her edition of his *Poems* (1797). In her will she writes:

> I bequeath if they will be pleased to accept of it [,] they having one already [,] the fine magnificent picture of my Father-in-Law Bp Berkeley [,] to the Provost and Fellows of Dublin College — painted by Vanderbank which with the frame cost five hundred pounds.

The fountain-motif in the background represents — as in the title-page of *Alciphron* — the abandonment of the Bermuda project and of God (see No. 41).

54. BERKELEY AND THE LIVING WATERS

Oil on canvas.
49″ × 40½″.

ARTIST: John Vanderbank?
Luce No. 7.
LOCATION: Trinity College, Dublin.
LITERATURE: Luce, 1949; Kerslake letter, 12 Aug. 1985.

THE BACKGROUND of this portrait duplicates the first *Alciphron* vignette (see No. 41).

It is unclear whether this portrait is the original of the Skelton engraving, No. 53, for although Eliza intended her Vanderbank for Trinity College in 1797, the present portrait was acquired by the College in 1870; hence it is uncertain whether it is the original of the engraving or merely a copy (see No. 55). In a private communication John Kerslake comments:

> I am doubtful about the attribution to Vanderbank, at any rate from what I can see from the photos, and assuming that the picture has not been altered in appearance by restoration — it doesn't look like it, but one needs to see the actual paint, rather than a photo. I can't think of an obvious attribution, though it might be worth bearing in mind Bindon, who painted Abp. Boulter. On the other hand, John Ingamells, the Director of the Wallace collection and author of a Mellon publication on portraits of *English* bishops (Berkeley not included) says that the composition reminds him of Vanderbank (though not the handling of the paint I would say). But the formula is one in vogue for episcopal portraits of about that day and used by other painters as well.

Professor Anne Crookshank agrees with Kerslake.

54

55. BERKELEY AND THE LIVING WATERS (Copy)

Oil on canvas.

ARTIST: Johann Zoffany?
LOCATION: Unknown.
LITERATURE: Kerslake, 1977.
Auctioned at Sotheby's, 4 Oct. 1967.

55

THIS PORTRAIT was unknown to Luce. It would seem to be a copy of the Trinity College portrait (No. 54). Since an artist would be less likely to make a copy of a copy, we suspect that the Trinity College portrait is the original Vanderbank from which the Skelton engraving (No. 53) was done. If so, then Skelton took considerable liberties.

56

GEORGE BERKELEY D.D.
Fellow 1707, Bishop of Cloyne 1733

56. BISHOP BERKELEY

Oil on canvas. c.1737-1738.
29" × 24".

ARTIST: James Latham.
Luce No. 9.
LOCATION: Trinity College, Dublin.
LITERATURE: Luce, 1949; Kerslake, 1977; Crookshank and the Knight of Glin, 1978.
Purchased by Trinity College, Dublin, 1865, for 20 guineas.

THIS IS PROBABLY the last of the contemporary Berkeley portraits. Latham was an Irishman from Tipperary, who practised in Dublin from the late 1720s until 1747. It was possibly painted during Berkeley's stay in Dublin from October 1737 to May 1738, or perhaps in the summer of 1746.

As Kerslake notes, the characteristic skin defect or wen in the inner corner of the right eye is particularly in evidence in this portrait, although it is also apparent in two portraits by Smibert, Nos. 10 and 20.

57. DR. GEORGE BERKELEY

Bishop of Cloyne.
After Latham (No. 56).
Mezzotint, c.1750.
14″ × 10″.

ENGRAVER: John Brooks.
LOCATION: National Library of Ireland.
LITERATURE: Prior, 1746; Luce, 1949; Crookshank and the
Knight of Glin, 1978.

THIS MEZZOTINT was a key to the identification of Latham's portraits in that none of them was signed. Since the mezzotint ascribed the painting (No. 56) to Latham, it made possible the identification of other Latham paintings (e.g. No. 24).

The inscription at the bottom of the mezzotint is to be explained, as Luce points out, by Prior's *Authentick Narrative of the Success of Tar-water* (1746), where Prior reports the case of John Brooks. As it gives some idea of Berkeley's tar-water, we quote it here:

> 133. *The Case of Mr.* John Brooks *Engraver, living at the Sign of Sir* Isaac Newton's *Head, on* Cork-Hill, Dublin; *communicated by him to* Thomas Prior, *Esq; on the 22nd of* June, 1745.
>
> The said Mr. *Brooks* was, in *November* 1744, seized with Stitches, and a pleuritic Fever which continued eight or ten Days; he was blooded once and became better, but going abroad too soon, caught Cold and relapsed, and was much worse than before, being seized with more violent Stitches, Oppression on his Chest, Difficulty of Breathing, with most profuse Sweatings so weakened him in some time, that he was reduced to Skin and Bone, without any Appetite or Rest, so that it was thought he could not live an Hour, as he could hardly draw his Breath; he was advised to go out of Town to the Park, and drink Tar-water, which he did at the Rate of three Pints a Day, for ten Days, warm, going to Bed, and getting up, and cold at other Times, at eight different Times a Day; along with which he only took thin Gruel, or Chickenbroth; at the End of Ten Days as he was able to go abroad, mending every Day, the Tar-water having removed his Stitches, Sweatings, and made him breathe as free as ever. He was advised to ride, which he did, and on the first Day of riding an Imposthume broke, which lay upon his Lungs; the first thing thrown up was a Bag which contained the impostumated Matter, which was followed by a great Discharge of corrupted Stuff mixed with Blood: he was immediately seized with a violent Spitting of Blood, which continued seven Days, and was blooded, but still continued to drink the Tar-water as before, which he found to heal his Lungs, and stop his Spitting of Blood, and in a Fortnight's Time got into so good a State of Health as to be able to pursue his Business; he is now as well as ever he was, his Spirits and Appetite rather better than at any Time before, and he still continues to drink Half a Pint every Morning.

Dr GEORGE BERKELEY,
Bishop of Cloyne.

Printed for J. Hinton, at the Kings Arms in Paternoster Row.

58. UNIVERSAL MAGAZINE ENGRAVING
Steel engraving, 1776.
5.6½″ × 3.4″.
LOCATION: Trinity College, Dublin.
LITERATURE: Luce, 1949.

THIS ENGRAVING from the *Universal Magazine,* December 1776, is after the original painting by Latham (No. 56), or possibly after the mezzotint by Brooks (No. 57) who benefitted from tar-water.

59. BERKELEY CARICATURE

1762.

2¼″ × 4⅛″.

ENGRAVER: Aveline.
LOCATION: Trinity College, Dublin.
LITERATURE: Luce, 1949; Berman, 1985 (b).

THIS CARICATURE was probably based on the mezzotint (No. 57) after the Latham portrait (No. 56). It accompanies the *British Plutarch* (1762) essay by Oliver Goldsmith. The caricature of Berkeley reflects Goldsmith's essay, at least as Luce reads it. He describes it as:

> . . . a slight, chatty pretentious and irresponsible account without any attempt at documentation. . . . Here almost certain is the source of the general misconception of the Man.

Luce did not know that the author of the biography was Goldsmith, whose uncle was Dean of Cloyne when Berkeley was Bishop. For this and other reasons Goldsmith's memoir cannot so easily be dismissed.

Aveline sculp.

Berkley B.^p of Cloyne

60. WEEKLY MAGAZINE ENGRAVING
1759-60.

ENGRAVER: Unknown.
Not listed in Luce.
LOCATION: Huntington Library, California.
LITERATURE: Berman, 1985 (b).

THIS ENGRAVING appeared with the original printing of the memoir by Goldsmith (see No. 59). It is possibly based on the Lambeth Palace Portrait (No. 47). The only extant copy of the engraving would seem to be in the Huntington Library, San Marino, California.

60

The Rev.ᵈ D.ʳ George Berkeley.

61. LETTER TO DR. BRACKSTONE
1750.

LOCATION: Trinity College, Dublin.
LITERATURE: *Works*, 1956-57; Keynes, 1976; Berman and Berman, 1982.

THIS LETTER CONTAINS a recipe for tar-water and provides a sample of Berkeley's handwriting. The letter is printed in *Works*, 1956, pp. 303-4.

In 1744 Berkeley wrote a poem, "On Tar", which sketches part of the argument in his *Siris: a Chain of Philosophical Reflexions and Inquiries concerning Tar-water* (1744); Here are some of the lines:

Hail vulgar juice of never-fading pine!
Cheap as thou art, thy virtues are divine.
To shew them and explain (such is thy store)
There needs much modern and much ancient lore.
While with slow pains we search the healing spell,
Those sparks of life, that in thy balsam dwell,
From lowest earth by gentle steps we rise
Through air, fire, aether to the highest skies.
Things gross and low present truth's sacred clue.
Sense, fancy, reason, intellect pursue
Her winding mazes, and by Nature's laws
From plain effects trace out the mystic cause,
And principles explore, though wrapt in shades,
That spring of life which this great world pervades,
The spirit that moves, the Intellect that guides,
Th' eternal One that o'er the Whole presides.
Causes connected with effects supply
A golden chain, whose radiant links on high
Fix'd to the sovereign throne from thence depend
And reach e'en down to tar the nether end.

It is noteworthy that in this poem Berkeley appears to connect tar-water and God with a "spring of life"; for the image of a spring, or fountain, appears throughout his works and portraits: at the end of the *Three Dialogues* (No. 9), in the *Proposal* (No. 15), in the cluster of Bermuda items (Nos. 20, 26-28, 41-42, 53-55). In his *Second Letter to Prior on Tar-water* (1746) Berkeley also speaks of:

The virtue of tar-water flowing like the Nile* from a secret and occult source, brancheth into innumerable channels, conveying health and relief, wherever it is applied. . .

*The Nile was by the Ancient Egyptians called *Siris*, which word also signifies, in Greek, a chain, though not so commonly used as *Sira*.

62

62. EXAMINATION HALL PORTRAIT OF BERKELEY

Oil on canvas, c.1783.

109″ × 69″.

ARTIST: Robert Home.

Luce No. 12.

LOCATION: Examination Hall, Trinity College, Dublin.

LITERATURE: Luce, 1949; Berman, 1985 (b).

THIS LARGE decorative painting in the Examination Hall of Trinity College, Dublin was one of several portraits of eminent Trinity men commissioned by the College and painted by Home between 1783 and 1788. Luce describes it as the ''. . . stage philosopher peering into infinity''.

63. **RECUMBENT FIGURE OF BERKELEY**
1880.

ARTIST: A. Bruce Joy.
LOCATION: Memorial Chapel, St. Colman's Cathedral, Cloyne, County Cork.
LITERATURE: Luce, 1949.

THIS MEMORIAL figure of Berkeley is at the centre of a memorial room in St. Colman's Cathedral, Cloyne. It was endowed partly by citizens of Rhode Island.

64. BERKELEY MEDAL FOR GREEK

Gold.

Diameter 1¾".

LOCATION: J. V. Luce, Dublin.

LITERATURE: Luce, 1949; McDowell and Webb, 1982; Berman, 1985 (a).

Designed and endowed by Berkeley for the best Greek essay at Trinity College.

64

BERKELEY FOUNDED the Gold Medal in Greek in 1735. Initially he distributed one or two of the medals annually at his own expense. Shortly before he died, he endowed the award in perpetuity. The horse is the Pindaric race horse; the Greek motto means "always to excel".

The medal here reproduced was awarded to Professor J. V. Luce of Trinity College, the son of A. A. Luce (see Nos. 65 and 66).

65. DE VALERA AND LUCE

In the *Irish Press*.
Photograph 1953.
LITERATURE: *Works*, 1953; Berman, 1977.

BERKELEY'S CONCERN for the economic and social welfare of Ireland was most evident in his *Querist* (1735-37), where, for example, he asked:

> Whether there ever was, is, or will be, an industrious nation poor, or an idle rich?
> Whether an uneducated gentry be not the greatest of national evils?
> Whether the true idea of money, as such, be not altogether that of a ticket or counter?
> Whether, if our ladies drank tea out of Irish ware, it would be an insupportable national calamity?
> Whether there can be a greater reproach on the leading men and the patriots of a country, than that the people should want employment?
> And whether methods may not be found to employ even the lame and the blind, the dumb, the deaf and the maimed?
> Whether, if the arts of sculpture and painting were encouraged among us, we might not furnish our houses?
> Whose fault is it if poor Ireland continues poor?

More than any of Berkeley's works, the *Querist* captured the sympathy of Berkeley's nationalist countrymen. Among its admirers were Charles O'Conor, John Mitchel and Eamon De Valera. Although Berkeley's attitude to his Catholic countrymen was by modern standards not entirely free of prejudice, he did favour admission of Catholics to Trinity College, Dublin, and

TRIBUTE TO PHIL(

George Berkeley was a Great Irishman, Taoiseach Declares

"GEORGE BERKELEY was one of the few who, in the truly dark and evil days in the history of our country, though himself exempt from the disabilities and suffering of the large majority of the people, sympathised with that majority of the people and tried to improve their condition."

So declared the Taoiseach, Mr. de Valera, when he opened an exhibition in Trinity College Library, yesterday, in connection with the bi-centenary commemoration of the death of the Irish philosopher.

The Taoiseach said he did not know whether Berkeley knew the Irish language, but he knew it was the language of the majority of the Irish people of his time. He thought it would not be out of place, therefore, to declare the exhibition open formally in Irish. He then said: "Fógraim an teasbáinteas so ar fhosgailt anois."

Mr. de Valera, addressing the representatives of universities and colleges from all parts of the world, said that the invitation gave him an opportunity, which he much desired, of being associated with the commemoration of a great Irishman.

Because of his work for the suffering majority of the people of Ireland in his day, Berkeley would be cherished forever by Irishmen. He would stand with men like Swift and Molyneux who, through a deep sense of justice and love for the land in which they were born, transcended the barriers which

The Taoiseach, Mr. de Valera, with Dr. A. A. Luce, M.A., Litt.D., at T.C.D., yesterday.

A BERKELEY DESCENDANT

PRESENT when the Taoiseach opened the George Berkeley bi-centenary exhibition in Trinity College yesterday, was another George Berkeley, a descendant of the philosopher's brother.

He was a close friend of the late Erskine Childers and during the Howth gun-running was organiser for the National Volunteers, and a member of the Gun Running Committee. On Tuesday he paid a visit to Wicklow and called on Mrs. Childers and Mr. Robert Barton.

SEEK HIGHER
CHARGES FOR

some expedient relaxation of the penal laws. He considered himself an Irishman, and this appealed to men as different as De Valera and Yeats.

De Valera delivered a speech at Cloyne on 7 June 1953, at the 200th anniversary of Berkeley's death, in which he praised the *Querist*.

66. A. A. LUCE AND E. J. FURLONG
Photograph, c.1935.

66

A. A. LUCE, preeminent Berkeley scholar, and his successor as Professor of Moral Philosophy at Trinity College, E. J. Furlong, who also wrote widely on Berkeley.

67

67. BERKELEY COMMEMORATIVE STAMP

Stamp designed by Brendan Donegan.
$1^1/_{16}''$ × $1^7/_{16}''$.
LITERATURE: *Irish Philatelic Bulletin,* June 1985.

THE STAMP WAS issued by the Irish Post Office on 20 June 1985 to mark the 300th anniversary of Berkeley's birth. It is after the portrait by Latham (No. 56).

REFERENCES

BERKELEY, Eliza. "Will", Trinity College, Dublin, MS 3530.

BERKELEY, George. *The Works of George Berkeley, Bishop of Cloyne,* edited by A. A. Luce and T. E. Jessop. London: Thomas Nelson and Sons; abbreviated as *Works*

Vol. 1	1948	Vol. 4	1951	Vol. 7	1955
Vol. 2	1949	Vol. 5	1953	Vol. 8	1956
Vol. 3	1950	Vol. 6	1953	Vol. 9	1957

BERMAN, David. "Berkeley, Clayton and *An Essay on Spirit",* *Journal of the History of Ideas* 1971, XXXII, 3.

BERMAN, David, "Mrs. Berkeley's annotations in her interleaved copy of *An Account of the life of George Berkeley* (1776)", *Hermathena,* Summer 1977, CXXII.

BERMAN, David "A Note on Berkeley and his Catholic Countrymen", *Long Room,* 1978.

BERMAN, David. "A New Berkeley Portrait", *Berkeley Newsletter,* No. 2, 1978.

BERMAN, David. "Berkeley's Prophecy", *The Scriblerian.* XIII No. 1, Autumn 1980.

BERMAN, David and BERMAN, Jill. "The Fountain Portraits of Bishop Berkeley", *Apollo,* February 1982, CXV.

BERMAN, David. "Berkeley and King", *Notes and Queries* 1982, New Series, Vol. 29, No. 6.

BERMAN, David. "George Berkeley: Irish Idealist", *Ireland Today* 1985, No. 1019.

BERMAN, David and BERMAN, Jill. "Berkeley's *Alciphron* Vignettes," *The Book Collector,* Spring 1985, Vol. 32, No. 1.

BERMAN, David. "George Berkeley (1685-1753): Pictures by Goldsmith, Yeats and Luce", *Hermathena* 1985 (b).

BERMAN, David. "The Jacobitism of Berkeley's *Passive Obedience",* forthcoming in the *Journal of the History of Ideas* 1986.

DRAYTON, Alice. *George Berkeley in Newport.* Newport, Rhode Island, 1954.

CLARK, Desmond. *Thomas Prior, 1681-1751.* Dublin: Royal Dublin Society, 1951.

CROOKSHANK, Anne and The Knight of Glin. *The Painters of Ireland 1660-1920.* Barrie & Jenkins Communic-Europa, London, 1978.

DOWNING, Antoinette F. and SCULLY, Vincent J. Jnr. *The Architectural Heritage of Newport, Rhode Island,* 2nd edition. New York: Bramhall House, 1967.

GAUSTAD, Edward. *George Berkeley in America.* New Haven: Yale University Press, 1979.

GOODWIN, Daniel. Editor, *A Letter Book and Abstract of Our Services 1743-1751.* Boston: The Merrymount Press, 1899.

HARDMAN, Edward T. "On Two New Deposits of Human and Other Bones, Discovered in the Cave of Dunmore, Co. Kilkenny," *Proceedings of the Royal Irish Academy,* April 1875, Vol. 2, Series 2, No. 2.

FOOTE, Henry Wilder. *John Smibert, Painter.* Cambridge: Harvard University Press, 1950.

FRASER, A. C. *The Life and Letters of Berkeley, D.D.*; Oxford:

Clarendon Press, 1871.

Irish Philatelic Bulletin, Dublin, 20 June 1985.

JAMES, Sydney V. *Colonial Rhode Island.* New York: Charles Scribner's Sons, 1975.

KERSLAKE, John. *Early Georgian Portraits.* 2 Vols. London: National Portrait Gallery, 1977.

KERSLAKE, John. Unpublished letter, 12 Aug. 1985.

KEYNES, Geoffrey. *A Bibliography of George Berkeley, Bishop of Cloyne.* Oxford: Clarendon Press, 1976.

LUCE, A. A. "Berkeley's Bermuda Project and His Benefactions to American Universities, with Unpublished Letters and Extracts from the Egmont Papers''. *Proceedings of the Royal Irish Academy,* August 1934, Vol. XLII, Section C, No. 6.

LUCE, A. A. "The Purpose and Date of Berkeley's Commonplace Book." *Proceedings of the Royal Irish Academy,* February, 1943, Vol. XLVIII, Section C, No. 1.

LUCE, A. A. *Life of George Berkeley, Bishop of Cloyne.* London: Thomas Nelson and Sons, 1949.

McDOWELL, R. B. and WEBB, D. A. *Trinity College Dublin 1592-1952, An Academic History.* Cambridge: Cambridge University Press, 1982.

MASON, George Champlin. *Annals of Trinity Church, Newport, Rhode Island,* 1698-1821. Newport, Rhode Island: George C. Mason, 1890.

MAXWELL, Constantia. *A History of Trinity College Dublin 1591-1892.* Dublin: The University Press, 1946.

O'LOINGSIGH, Padraigh. Editor, *The Book of Cloyne.*

Middleton: Cloyne Historical and Archaeological Society, 1977.

PRIOR, Thomas. *An Authentick Narrative of the Success of Tar-Water.* London-printed, W. Innys, etc., 1746.

RAND, Benjamin. *Berkeley and Percival.* Cambridge: Cambridge University Press, 1914.

SAUNDERS, Richard Henry. *John Smibert (1688-1751): Anglo-American Portrait Painter,* 2 Vols. Ann Arbor: University Microfilms International, 1979.

SMIBERT, John. *The Notebook of John Smibert. With essays by Sir David Evans, John Kerslake and Andrew Oliver and Notes relating to Smibert's American portraits by Andrew Oliver.* Boston: Massachusetts Historical Society, 1969.

STOCK, Joseph. *Account of the Life of George Berkeley.* London, 1776.

STRICKLAND, W. G. *A Descriptive Catalogue of the Pictures . . .in Trinity College, Dublin.* The University Press, 1916.

TUVESON, E. L. *Redeemer Nation: The Idea of America's Millennial Role.* Chicago, 1968.

UPDIKE, Wilkins. *Memoirs of the Rhode Island Bar.* Boston: Thomas H. Webb, 1842.

UPDIKE, Wilkins. *A History of the Episcopal Church in Narragansett.* Boston: Merrymount Press, 1847.

A Visit to Historic Trinity Church in Newport. Newport, Rhode Island: Trinity Church, 1973.

ACKNOWLEDGEMENTS

1. John Brooks; 2. David Berman; 3. National Library of Ireland; 4. David Berman; 5. Ramie Leahy; 6. *Irish Times*; 7. National Library of Ireland; 8. and 9. Board of Trinity College, Dublin; 10. Mrs. Maurice Berkeley; 11. Board of Trinity College, Dublin; 12. National Gallery of Ireland; 13. National Library of Ireland; 14. Zeitlin and Ver Brugge; 15. Board of Trinity College, Dublin; 16. National Library of Ireland; 17. W. Bartlett; 18. and 19. Board of Trinity College, Dublin; 20. National Portrait Gallery, London; 21. Massachusetts Historical Society; 22. Photo Gordon Rowley, courtesy R. Houghton, M. Lapan, R. McKenna; 23. and 24. Representative Church Body; 25. Photo K. Ed Kelly, Bermuda Historical Society; 26. National Gallery of Ireland; 27. Yale University Art Gallery, New Haven, gift of Isaac Lathrop; 28. Photo Brendan Dempsey; 29. Newport Historical Society; 30. R. Houghton; 31. Trinity Church, Newport; 32. M. Lapan; 33. Redwood Library and Athenaeum; 34. David Berman; 35. Columbia University in the City of New York; 36. Bowdoin College Museum of Art; 37. Photo M. Lapan; 38. W. Spencer Crooks; 39. National Gallery of Ireland; 40. Newport Historical Society; 41. and 42. David Berman; 43. Rhode Island Development Council; 44. and 45. R. Houghton; 46. Board of Trinity College, Dublin; 47. Archbishop of Canterbury: Copyright reserved by Courtauld Institute and the Church Commissioners; 48. David Berman; 49. Trustees of the Late Lord Berkeley, Berkeley Castle; 50. David Berman; 51. R. Houghton; 52. National Library of Ireland; 53. Marsh's Library, Dublin; 54. Board of Trinity College, Dublin; 56. Board of Trinity College, Dublin; 57. National Library of Ireland; 58. and 59. Board of Trinity College, Dublin; 60. Huntington Library, California; 61. and 62. (photo by B. Dempsey) Board of Trinity College, Dublin; 63. R. Houghton; 64. J. V. Luce; 65. *Irish Press*; 66. B. Dempsey; 67. An Post.

NOTES ON THE AUTHORS

DR. RAYMOND W. HOUGHTON is Research Associate at Trinity College, Dublin, and President of the International Berkeley Society.

DR. DAVID BERMAN, F.T.C.D., is a Senior Lecturer in the Philosophy Department at Trinity College, Dublin; he is Editor of the *Berkeley Newsletter.*

DR. MAUREEN LAPAN is Professor of Foundations of Education at Rhode Island College, and Historian of the International Berkeley Society.